Eyes of the Heart

Eyes of the Heart

More Best Loved Sermons

by

William E. Nebo

Sursum Corda Press
Livermore, California

Editing by Claudia McCormick
Book Design by Judy Lussie
Cover Design and Photo by Charles Eyler

PRINTED IN THE UNITED STATES OF AMERICA

ISBN 978-0-9799929-1-9

Library of Congress Control Number: 2008939137

This book is dedicated to Henrietta Greer and her husband, the late Tom Greer, my spiritual parents and grandparents to my family during our life in Livermore.

Table of Contents

Preface

The first book of Bill Nebo's sermons, The Soul's Journey, was published November 2007. It was such a huge success that we were encouraged to print a second book. The two books represent 57 of the 106 sermons that we selected for possible publication.

When Rev. William "Bill" Nebo announced he would be retiring from the ministerial staff of the First Presbyterian Church in Livermore, CA, many church members began reminiscing about their favorite sermons. It was not uncommon to hear "I liked that sermon about the weed whacker, " or "After all these years, my son still remembers the sermons about Bill as a child."

Hearing these comments and knowing that Bill would no longer be delivering sermons at our church we proceeded to publish our favorite sermons. The original review committee included: Claude and Peggy Burdick, Edward and Connie Clark, Jim and Janie Hodges, Bill and Judy Lussie, Art Rodrigues, Robbie See, and Ann Laye

With the help of the church staff, particularly Penny Kammeijer, Joy Fischer and Michele O'Hair, we scanned and copied 526 sermons dating back to 1981. Members of our committee read and ranked sermons which were selected as possible for publication.

We are grateful to members of our committee who served as copy editors. This group included: Claude Burdick, Peggy Burdick, Robbie See, and Larry Burdick.

We thank three special individuals who are primarily responsible for the publications: Claudia McCormick who served proficiently as the content editor and Judy and Bill Lussie who served as the mainstay in the publishing phase of this project.

Finally, we wish to thank Chuck Eyler for the photography and cover design for both publications, including the picture of Bill reading to his granddaughter for this book.

It is our hope that these best loved sermons of Bill Nebo will be enjoyed for many years by present and future generations.

Marvin and Mary V. Dickerson,
Sermon Project Co-chairs

Introduction

Tom and Henrietta Greer were aware of many fences that needed mending in the First Presbyterian Church of Livermore when I became its senior pastor in 1976. They decided that what people needed to do was see each other anew through the eyes of friendship and Christian tolerance. To do this they organized a number of dinners over several years. They invited people of varying degrees of experience in the congregation, mixing in both the disgruntled with the satisfied. Each time we had a dinner Henrietta and Tom told me and my wife, Jean, a little about each guest, as much as they knew, and then seated me near those who had some negative feelings about the church or its pastors.

The ground rules of the night were always spelled out by Tom. No political or religious arguments were to be aired at the gathering, it was just fellowship. But strangely enough, by the end of the dinner people who had been cross-wise politically or religiously were again enjoying each other's company.

I was one of those who saw people differently after those dinners than when I checked out the guest list. Tom and Henrietta helped me see with the "eyes of the heart" and for that I am forever grateful.

I am grateful for the loving use of those "eyes of the heart" by those who shaped this book. I am especially sensitive about oversights of attribution I may have lost during my creation of weekly sermons. Hopefully, the sources will forgive me and enjoy the respect shown in their use.

I pray that all those who read these sermons and sermon excerpts will find greater clarity given to their "eyes of the heart".

Rev. William E. Nebo

Thanksgiving's Zoom Lens

November 24, 1985

Paul had much on his mind when he wrote the introduction to I Corinthians. The situation was volatile in Corinth. Paul's name was being deployed as a weapon by one group of people and an object of ridicule by another. He was distressed to hear about the turmoil in the Corinth church that had once shown such great promise. There was more than a little annoyance in Paul against the people he believed were stirring up trouble and making what Paul discerned were wrong-headed decisions and statements.

If we were given the assignment to write a letter to this difficult group, we would probably get right to the point: "Dear Friends in Corinth: How dare some of you malign me as you have. Shape up or ship out. Love, Mr. and Ms. High Authority."

Paul once wrote a letter of that type to the Galatian church. I notice that he never repeated the mistake.

Instead, Paul begins this letter with a set of thanksgivings for the very people he is later going to chastise. I suppose one could say that Paul was just buttering up his audience for the roasting he would give them later. He was using sweet talk to keep them reading until he could get in the swift kick.

However, that explanation is too trifling. Except for Galatians, Paul began each of his letters with a similar thanks to God for the positive characteristics of his fellow pilgrims, whether or not he had harsh things to say.

Paul was sending up prayers of thanks which Jesus frequently offered before he acted. For example, before Jesus raised Lazarus from the dead, he offered a prayer of thanksgiving. That appeared strange to the onlookers. One would think, given his situation, he would be asking for every particle of power he could summon, rather than giving thanks for something not yet accomplished.

Likewise one might expect Paul to be praying for the church's rectification at the outset of his letter to Corinth.

Henri Nouwen, in his book, *Gracias: A Latin American Journal*, gives us a clue to why Paul has this preference for thanksgiving. Nouwen writes of a visit to Bolivia in 1981 saying,

> During the last few days my thoughts kept moving around the significance of gratitude (or thanksgiving) in mission work. Gratitude is becoming increasingly important for those who

want to bring the good news of the kingdom to others. For a long time, the predominant attitude of the missionaries was that they had to bring the knowledge of the Gospel to poor, ignorant people and thus offer light in their darkness. In such a view there is not much room for gratitude. As the missionary attitude changed, however, and more and more missionaries came to see their task as helping others to recognize their own God given talents and thus to claim the good news for themselves, gratitude became much more than an occasional "Thanks be to God."

Nouwen helps us to see that giving thanks to God for specific people helps us to focus on those people in a positive way. This sort of thanksgiving starts with the premise that God has a unique love and purpose for every human soul. He blesses each with certain gifts, which are valuable to that soul and to the community in which the single soul finds identity.

Thanksgiving and praise change the way we look at people. Its presence can make their gifts real for us, and its absence can cause us to totally miss the value of their contribution.

Football coaches know all about this power of praise and thanksgiving. They know that if they go on television thankful for the fact that the quarterback has developed some extra long passing skill in the last month, or that the line backers have developed an esprit and bond which made them into tigers on defense, the coaches know it will change the way the opponent looks at the team. Conversely, the coaches will try to affect the opponents' expectations of the team with a lot of trouble talk. Such as, "Well, we're seeing a lot of problems with injuries and I just hope that our quarterback will still be able to hit the line with a pass in the second quarter."

The act of giving thanks helps us to focus on the God given gifts, the special graces in a situation. Nouwen discovered that when he and other missionaries began to give praise and thanksgiving to God for what was already there in their people, they found these gifts coming to fruition. The act of thanksgiving became an agent in identifying God's hidden gifts in others, and then bringing these gifts out for discovery and positive use by the individual and the community.

Nouwen also discovered that as one focused on a person with thanksgiving to God, one was led to discover even more subtle, yet perhaps grander talents and gifts that were not first apparent from a mere precursory assessment of the individual.

Giving God praise for what He graciously gives to us is like a zoom lens, focusing us on the positive potentials God built into life everywhere.

Paul sought to relate to the health of those he wrote to. He availed himself of the power of contemplative thanksgiving, feeling out the places in their souls where God had blessed them with great wholeness and health. Holding these before him like a light, he plunged into the confusion of the conflict, which was constraining the use of these gifts. Paul sought to unlock God's love, goodness, unity, and power in a warring congregation. He approached it honestly, confrontationally, but he did so having focused his vision on its gifts rather than its liabilities.

This gratitude that we see in Paul and hear described by Nouwen is not just thanksgiving at the time of year when the holiday is celebrated. It should be a tradition of perpetual thanksgiving. If we are to have the power that thanksgiving can unlock, we must use it continually and at every level of life. We must focus it daily on our spouses, our children and family, our co-workers, our opponents, our neighbors, our national and international relationships. As we do we will find more and more to be thankful for in each of these arenas of life.

Many of us have had an experience called Marriage Encounter. That experience has proven for many of us a total renewal of the love and appreciation between our spouses and us. It succeeds because the experience concentrates on thanksgiving and praise for one's marital mate. As wives and husbands recognize and verbalize and are thankful for each other's gifts, a whole string of unexplored, unappreciated gifts come to light in the relationship.

Thanksgiving isn't an indulgence or a sign of good manners. The act of giving thanks is a God directed and God given tool for uncovering the power He has placed in a multiplicity of gifts in our lives. It is conscious scanning radar that seeks high peaks of latent power in curious places.

Give thanks to God. Focus the zoom lens of your vision and receive a spectacular display of His ability to bless those who diligently seek Him.

My football days

Messy Lines in Faithful Minds

February 19, 2006

Whenever a completely regular form appears in nature we are suspicious that humans have made it. That is because things tend to have fuzzy edges, unclean boundaries, and irregular outlines in nature. Looking down from space and seeing a straight as stick marking usually means, "man made". Seeing something under water (during a deep water dive) that rises up from the bottom with straight sides exactly parallel or circular means that it is of human origin. This makes me think that in the scheme of things the creator's plan was to have the really clean, uncluttered things inhabit the minds of humans instead of the created order. Maybe that was because humans have to begin with the uncluttered in order to deal with the cluttered world in which God nestles the real significant meaning and mysteries of why we are really here.

Paul was a man of great energy and high expectations. His passion for sharing the gospel struck up the fire of faith in the world beyond the Judaism in which Christianity was born so that it came of age as a multi-cultured faith instead of a belief system of a single culture. But this meant that it was harder for anyone to manage it and control it because it didn't travel along a straight line of sight created by one or a few people's minds.

Paul liked lines that had neat, controlled and predictable beginnings and ends. When people working with him deviated from those lines he had drawn about doctrine, or strategy, or assessments of others, it was hard for him to compromise. It was hard for him to repaint the bright pictures he had in his head, once he painted them in his lofty, bold colors.

The other day I was golfing with a friend. We were supposed to tee off at 7:50 a.m. but when we arrived a large group of men in several foursomes had already teed off and were planning to stream out onto the course, a foursome at time until 9 a.m. We explained that we were supposed to have been ahead of them.

One of their number who was in the next foursome warmly invited us to just jump into the stream ahead of them. He said that he couldn't see any reason why it would make any great difference to anyone. I explained that at least I wasn't a very great golfer and could be slow. He laughed and said neither were any of their foursomes and we would fit right in and cause no noticeable back up that amounted to anything.

We both felt pretty warmly received and also disposed to try to make the day a good one for this spirit. So we insisted on first seeing if the golf course had another course we could start on so we wouldn't be in their way. Our inquiries revealed that no other course was available. The manager told us to simply start on the second hole ahead of the next foursome and end the day with hole one as our last hole. He offered to go with us to tell the group that this was how it needed to be. We declined the offer. We wanted the gracious amiability we had met at the starting hole to continue.

But when we returned the original foursome had golfed on and we met another foursome with a different spokesman. This man was irritated that we were there. We were a ragged edge to the world he had imagined ahead of his foursome and behind it. He sought to explain how our presence would completely throw off everything including the tilt of the earth. Neither of us believed a word he said. Both of us thought that reason had nothing to do with the picture of the day we simply did not fit in his mind's eye.

I considered getting the groundskeeper to force the man out of the way and get us started. But I remembered the warmth of the first encounter with the man who was focused on the fact that we were all just trying to have some fun and really had no great reason to make it fit tightly between the edges of a schedule. It was enough to remind me to be unencumbered by the straight lines of my interpretation of who had the "right of way" in the matter and to just let go of the issue and wait until 9 a.m. and start. And besides the man had just made clear to me what was happening in this scripture I had read for this morning's sermon.

It isn't easy to let go of our need for others to meet the pictures we paint of them in our heads. It means starting over, and that means rearranging other pictures, other evaluations, perhaps some self-evaluation. That brings some fear of self-confrontation, and the fear makes us hang on tighter. In fact we are often afraid to let go of these cartoon picture expectations of each other even though this hanging on is obviously destructive.

This reminds me of a story from my younger years as a youth pastor in San Francisco. We took a group of youths to work on reconstruction and remodeling of a rural neighborhood house in a place called Tracy California. In that year of 1968 Tracy was pretty small and centered on agriculture. One of our youngest workers was assigned the task of torching off some very large piles of brush we had piled into a field. Having given him clear instructions we left him to his task.

As rising smoke telegraphed the message that the burning had begun, an older youth came streaking over to me and in great agitation blurted out the news that my fire starter was stoking his fire by flinging gas on it from an open gas can. He was hardly finished speaking before I was flying to stop this foolishness. When I dashed around a comer of a building and spied the youth who had just flung a spray of gas into the flames I yelled his name. He turned around just as a line of flame flashed from the fire and into the can that immediately began spurting an impressive column of fire.

My agitated shouting at the youth to drop the can and run startled the youth. He glanced at the can, saw the fact that it had become a blowtorch and panicked. Instead of dropping the erupting gas can, he tried to fling it away from him with all of his might. But his fear over what he imagined coming only made him grip the can tighter so that he couldn't let go. So he danced wildly about flinging fire in every direction, trying to throw that can away until every drop of gas and every fume was gone from the can. It was only after the fiery fuel was exhausted that he finally found the will to let go of the can.

Hanging onto a need to see the world drawn in the regular shapes can find us dancing about in life spreading destructive fire everywhere just like that young man was dancing around unable to let go of what had become a fountain of fire.

God invites us to look at life through the lenses. His redeeming love that we witnessed in Jesus; lenses that don't need a life of straight lines, predictable angles, cleaned up surfaces and crisp, non-ragged edges in order to be at peace and to be an instrument of the peace that passes understanding.

May it be so among us. Amen

12

Saving the Present Time

October 21, 2001

Imagine yourself approaching a check-out counter at a store. A customer ahead of you is trying to tell the store clerk something about a purchase and is having trouble settling his issue with the clerk. The clerk is becoming annoyed. You don't really know the circumstances; you just know that the clerk reminds you of the way your dad used to get aggravated. You begin to interact with the present moment, running a film clip in your head of past encounters with your Dad. You think, *I know just what that poor guy is going through trying to tell that self-important clerk what he wants. My dad was just like that clerk, and I remember how he always heard what he wanted to hear, and that clerk is just as hard headed as my dad. He must be about dad's age when I had so much trouble with him. He even kind of looks like my dad 25 years ago. When it comes my turn to deal with the clerk I'm not taking any guff off of the idiot.*

It comes to be your turn; the clerk finishes up the paper work of the customer ahead of you, and says to you nicely, "Can I help you?"

And you say, "Don't fool with me buddy"

We can let our past infect the present with negative feelings it doesn't deserve. We can allow our past to lock us into attitudes which bend the present, so that the radiant possibilities of joy and redemption are cordoned off from us by hostility, arrogance, or ungracious judgment.

Equally, we can be distracted from the significance of God in the present moment, by too much obsession about the future. This happens, for example, when we are too taken up with plans we making to buy something, or create something, or change something. I remember trying to visit with a man who was concerned that his wife wanted to leave him. He told me he was heartbroken, and wanted to do everything he could to convince her that she was the love of his life and things would be different if she just consented to remain in their home.

He was a nice person, intelligent, successful and personable. He told me he was very busy at work, so I met him in the city at a restaurant frequented by the business people of the financial district. While we ate, he was constantly seeing people he knew and obviously felt compelled to network with by making some significant greeting. The fact is that I know we spoke about his marriage but all I remember is the many interruptions he made in our discussion to build for his business future by keeping his contacts with other alive and hot. The fact is, I was visiting with only half a person. The other half was busy with the future, missing the fact that he really couldn't be fully present to our conversation even when the conversation was ostensibly about what was of the greatest value to his life.

Too much attachment to the future causes us to be frantic, worried, distracted in the present, and distorted in our placement of value and use of time and energy.

Here is a good Sabbath practice sheet for you:

Somewhere in the day, spend time in absolute silence with God, shutting off your ego demands and concerns of the world. Start by counting your breath and paying attention only to that. Move to simple repeating of a mantra prayer like the "God, you are my refuge and help". You choose the words, but concentrate only on them. Let all other thoughts come and go. Don't fight them. Just stay as focused as possible for as long as you can. Increase this time until you reach between 30 minutes and one hour. You might wish to visualize God's presence as light filling your head and body, burning away pain, confusion, guilt and the like.

In the spirit of the Sabbath, do no work which involves changing things. Forget this if your water heater blows out and a stream of cold water is surging into your laundry room at street pressure. Short of such absolute necessities, spend a day not tinkering, or changing things. Spend the day being with and observing, perhaps writing in your journal. This includes not doing work on your kids or your family. Avoid educational advice for your spouse, who may not like it anyway. Avoid lecturing anyone for his or her edification. Think before you respond. Ask what response makes the Sabbath holy, joy filled. Avoid correcting anyone if possible. Avoid grumbling and complaining. Don't drink. It dulls your sense of the world you are supposed to be enjoying.

Try to get outside and notice the weather, the stages of life of plants and trees, and the presence of animals. Smell the air, notice changes in those smells as you walk. Take a walk and try to speak with as many people as you comfortably can. A kind, sincere greeting is sufficient often. Try to remember whom you saw. And as you see people, try not to judge and draw conclusions. You are there to experience God in people, not to usurp the place of God in judging them or changing their behavior. Be the walk-on in everyone else's stage production instead of the star of your own.

Speak to children you meet in your neighborhood. Start remembering their names, their stories, and their dramas. This is harder at some stages of their lives. Be aware of this and seek to overcome the judging which keeps you from relating without threat.

Visit your friends. In doing so beware of ego games like matching stories of success, or relating yet another time you were a hero of some tense drama. Prepare some jokes or stories for your friends' pleasure. Think of some sort of play that would bring all of you delight. Bring a musical instrument to play with your friends as long as it isn't going to get you into competitive stress.

Avoid the evening news and television which leaves you filled with ego pressure, competition, guilt about what you have or haven't done etc.

Well, you get the point. The Sabbath is something we build, not simply live through. It is a commitment we make to spending time with God by immersing ourselves in the wonderful gifts of God.

There is an old Sufi saying which says, "I laugh when I hear that the fish in the water are thirsty." It tells us that our thirst for the holy is easily satisfied, if we simply spend silent time with God and notice what is really and truly going on all around us and in us.

Amen.

Leaving Behind the Household Gods

June 5, 2005

U r of the Chaldese was one of the great cities of civilization of the ancient world in which Abraham and Sarah lived. It was located on the Euphrates River in Mesopotamia, now southern Iraq not far from the Persian Gulf. It was the happening place of the time, the place to be if one wanted to traffic in agriculture, or make it in real estate, commerce, or politics.

We speculate that Abraham and Sarah lived in Ur after a group of Semitic people called Amorites dominated the city state and overlaid its life with their culture. The mighty Hammurabi creator of the great law code of the ancient world was part of this influx of people into the Tigris/Euphrates river valley city state system that made ancient Mesopotamia what it was.

It appears that Abraham and Sarah had profited by their years in Ur. But despite their comfortable abundance in physical things, their lives were not aimed in the direction they really had wanted to go. Abraham and Sarah were not able to conceive children, try as they would. This meant that they had no heirs and no way to keep their family name alive - something that ancients connected with immortality.

So they prayed to the One True God Abraham and Sarah had found in the midst of the gods of the Sumerian-Amorite culture in which they lived. Perhaps it was while praying to find meaning in the life they had not expected to live that Abraham was told what he should do. He should get himself packed up and move out of Ur, and go to an unspecified place that he would recognize because God would help him discern it when he arrived. And by the way, leave behind the household gods - symbols of the city bound deities worshiped by so many.

This was an unsettling thing for ancient people used to city states. It was believed that the great gods inhabited the city states. One could travel to another locale and take along with him the household icons of the gods of the previous residence, but there was no guarantee that the god represented by the household god, would have power in the new locale. In that case one would have to discover what god had power to act in the new place.

Abraham and Sarah left behind the households of their upbringing and joined the streams of nomadic families, living from oasis to oasis. Their journey took them to the land of Canaan. It set them down in the midst of a land that was untouched by the law code of Hammurabi that did not possess cities made into states by great irrigation systems hooked to the powerful flow of water down the Euphrates and into the Persian Gulf. There was no protective wall and battle toughened city state military to protect them from raiders and roving bands of violent men. There was only the invisible presence that had set them on their way promising a blessing in an unspecified place and at an unspecified time.

Having arrived in Shechem the band of Abraham and Sarah's tribe paused at the great tree of Moreh. And that is where the invisible God appeared again. Again the promise was made. It must have been a great relief to Abraham to actually know that the God, who had pressed him to leave his familiar home, was waiting for him in every place he went as he sought his new home. It was a great comfort to know that God was not a god who could get out of touch should one take a wrong turn or travel beyond some limit of God's range of influence. Abraham's experience of God was that everywhere he wandered, looking for the place where he should settle God was there already waiting for him.

This story reminds us that God wants to be a partner in our spiritual trip through life, just as God sought to be a partner with Sarah and Abraham in their trip. God is a great companion. God doesn't jump off the bus if you drive it stupidly in the wrong direction, or take a weird detour that you could have avoided. God seems to relish the adventure of you driving and God advising, and even sometimes ordering, recognizing that plenty of God's children disobey orders. And when we arrive at all of our destinations in life, God is already there, waiting for us, ready to discuss the meaning of where we have arrived.

Of course we have to recognize the fact that what God has promised to us is not that we are the stars of the show. We are part of its unfolding drama but we aren't the drama. God tells us that it culminates in something tremendous, and to make it really stupendous there are some rules about how we should play our part in it. There are some directions to look at on the map in order to make progress in the journey so that those who follow us are left closer to the goal rather than farther away.

Abraham and Sarah were promised something they really didn't see. They eventually had Isaac, but only after Sarah had given up hope of ever conceiving and ordered that her maid Hagar be her husband's concubine and bear him a child. Then, Sarah was able to have only one child before she died. She did not live to participate in the arranged marriage of her son, which went forward directed by a servant rather than herself. Nor did she see the day when Isaac and his half brother who Sarah and Abraham had cast into the desert with their mother would come together as brothers to bury their father.

Grieving Abraham buried his wife. He married Keturah who bore him six sons, but Abraham never found it in himself to consider them equal with Isaac. So he gave them gifts when they were grown and sent them out to make their lives. He kept Isaac with him until his death and passed the family name and inheritance to him. The great expansion of his offspring would only happen generations after his two sons buried him in a cave in the field of Ephron, son of Zohar the Hittite.

By the time Abraham made his second major stop on his journey into his unfolding future, he had learned to pause and seek the counsel of God. By then he had learned that wherever he was, God was already there, waiting to be consulted.

So it is with us on life's journey. There are times when we leave one place in life and go to another and it seems as if we leave all that is familiar behind, including the comforting assurance that God is with us making meaning evident, or at least evident enough to keep it hopeful. This story says it isn't so. God is not only never left behind, but God awaits us in the next place we go to, patiently waiting until we quietly turn our attention to him, sort of build an altar as Abraham did, and say, "I know you're here, where do you suggest I go next."

When I left for college I left behind my mother and my step-father. I was so glad to get them out of my hair that I hardly said goodbye as I marched into the dorm building with my suitcase, declining their offer to accompany me to my room. But then, standing in the middle of the lobby, 17 years old and among the youngest of human beings bustling around in that place where everyone was as smart as or smarter than me, as accomplished as or more so than me, I suddenly lost all confidence. I had just wandered from familiar Ur where I knew the name of God, and into Canaan where I only had God's promise that if I asked God would be there.
I arrived at my room on the sixth floor thoroughly undone. I sat on my bed. It came to me that the assistant minister of my church whom I listened to with great attention had once told this story of Abraham, pointing out the promise was really that at every strange place we turn up in life, if we look, God will already be there. So I asked, what I would do if I were like Abraham, really thinking God was there. It came to

me; I would be a hospitable host the roommate who would soon arrive.

So I followed that lead. I made the bed of my roommate to be. I tidied up his towels, did some special things that said "Welcome" and waited. That small act of faith transformed my fright into glad anticipation. It was a huge relief. When my new roommate appeared we introduced ourselves and Barry Paschal looked about and said, "Who made my bed and put out all my towels?" I said I did. Barry looked really delighted and said, 'Thanks, I really appreciate that." Our friendship was born in that moment and launched me on a path that brought me into the warmest contact with the Jewish community of my life. Its lessons would go with me into my ministry for the rest of my working life.

There are many trips to Canaan from Ur awaiting us, trips in which we sort of leave behind the security of the household gods, and have to rely upon the real presence of the One True God. These journeys can be the journeys we take from employment into unemployment or the reverse: they can be the trip from marriage into being widowed or left a widower or the reverse: wealth and security into insecurity or the reverse; they can be the trip from a place of prestige to a place of anonymity and lack of influence; they can be trips from the opportunities of good health into the restrictions of ill health.

And if we treat all of these times of great change whether adverse or blessed as holy ground, God will appear in them when we "set up the altar" and call upon God's name.

Jane and I were married February 14, 2004

Separate Vacations for Me and Myself

July 8, 1984

We all want to pack it in during vacation~ I see my own coming in a few days. I am already beginning to look around for the ultimate recreation--the Great Big Fun--that will totally rejuvenate, totally restore, totally reinvigorate, and totally make all of life's toil during the rest of the year make sense. I know it is possible if only one thing is also possible that one thing is that I take a vacation from myself.

Impossible! We take ourselves on vacation, don't we, just like we take ourselves into our other mistaken panaceas--love affairs, new jobs or new positions~ new houses~ new children. We find the same trouble in the new setting, new clothes, and new relationship as the old one. We find ourselves looking for what it is in the setting that has us blocked, up tight, angry, and frustrated and we look in vain until we look into ourselves.

I had two friends in college who roomed next door to a fellow student whose final exams finished the first day of finals. He gloated over his good fortune to my friends, and partied loudly as way of rubbing in his good fortune (all in fun). So my friends took some extra time out and while their reveling neighbor was out of his room they picked his lock. Using great care they ran two tiny wires from their own stereo set in their room through a small hole in the adjoining corners of their rooms, and hooked the wires to the wires leading from their neighbors' stereo to his speakers.

Now I must tell you that this neighboring student had stereo speakers of great quality, locked into an upper closet area which he took great care to protect with two inch wood screws screwed into the door every few inches for added protection to prying fingers.

The next day my two friends left for their eight o'clock final. Their neighbor was sleeping off the effects of another night of post exam debauchery. Before leaving for their final, my friends put a John Phillips Souza march album on their stereo, and switched their speaker output switch to the wires leading to a their sleeping neighbors speakers. They turned the volume up to a robust number, flipped the needle onto the record and headed for the door.

Their neighbor of course leapt out of his skin when the "Stars and Stripes Forever" suddenly and unexplainably burst forth at ear splitting volume from his tightly secured speakers. Frantically he tore his stereo amplifier apart, taking every tube out. Just as frantically he took every lock and every wood screw out of his overhead cabinet while John Phillip Sousa gave him the most incredible headache that crashed like a rip tide against the already established headache of his previous night's revelry.

All during the episode, before he finally figured out what was going on, a voice in his brain kept screaming "Where is the noise coming from? Where is it coming from?"

In our lives we scurry around like that... ill at ease with our lot in life, unhappy, unfulfilled, with a voice inside saying where is all this unsettling noise in my life coming from? And just like the student next door to my friends, we look in the wrong places for the noise, and go to great lengths and expend great energy on the wrong jobs trying to get the noise to abate and find some peace.

So we go on vacations. The hard-driven, anxious business person, or scientist, or parent, or minister, gets the family into the car and declares that the vacation has begun and a destination has been selected where the promise of vacation peace will be realized. And in familiar style, the hard driver drives the whole family mad driving to the vacation.

"Let's not dally around, let's get organized and get this show onto the road now."

"No, we can't stop for a little hike along the river. We'll be late to the camp ground as it is."

"Can't you read a map, you've got us lost again."

"Of course, I'm upset. I only ask for you to pay attention to what you're doing so we don't lose time being lost."

Ah, yes! Familiar sounds of the stress that kills a vacation. It is all so familiar because even when we are on vacation, we take ourselves with us and the room full of noise and confusion that has harried our souls and plagued our spirits when we were not on vacation. We arrive at Nirvana Camp ground or where ever, still ill at ease, blaming others for our lack of peace or if we're more honest, just confused about where all the confusing noise in our lives is coming from.

I do not want to minimize the importance of external pressures on us. Poverty, illness, the cruelty and insensitivity of others who do hold some power over us can truly shape our lives.

But today's scripture from Romans reminds us that many times the noise of our lives is not coming from outside of ourselves. And when we tear round trying to turn it off dealing with externals, we are often not going to the real source of the noise.

So Paul admits to us that often he finds himself unable to do what he knows he ought to do in life. It makes him feel wretched, out of control, hypocritical, even a bit mad.

Paul has every reason to feel all of this. He was no saint in spite of our desire to make him one. His writing in Galatians and Corinthians is so full of his own egoism that he would probably blush to know that we were still reading it and trying to make something noble out of his angry outbursts that exist alongside the great wisdom of his calmer self.

And here in Romans he struggles with the reality that he, too, wishes he could take a vacation from himself at times, leaving behind the hurt Paul, the angry Paul, the defensive Paul, the insecure Paul, the Paul who thought of himself as ugly, the Paul who thought of himself as smart but not smart enough, the Paul who was prone to strike out at criticizers rather than listen to them, the Paul who thought his own ways were always better than the ways of others.

But we do not take vacations from ourselves. And we do not stop the noise in our lives when we are tearing about seeking to undo and fix and tear out the wrong things.

Paul says that the mind that is set on the flesh courts death and the mind that is set on the spirit courts life and peace. In short he says that the final solution to all of the noise pollution of our lives is to deal with it at the source, and the source is in our spirits, our deepest thoughts where our fears and hopes and fantasies are formed, and where faith and dread contend to decide who rules the light of day.

So if we go on vacation and hope to find peace away from ourselves by putting our bodies in another location for awhile, luxuriating in a pool in a resort for a few days or even weeks, we will be kidding ourselves. We will find ourselves simply putting our fingers in our ears against the noise of our souls and stopping the noise only temporarily. When we finally have to take our fingers from our ears to try to attend to life and our relationship, we will find ourselves bewildered by the same inner noise.

Peace is found when we seek God's healing in the midst of all the fragmented truths of who we are and what we are becoming. The hard driver finds that all of the organizing in the world is just another part of living in the flesh as Paul would have it unless he or she comes to grips with the fact that this organizing is an insane need to control, based on old fears and insecurities. The silent resenter, who finds every vacation another extended trip into being unappreciated, and unnoticed, works in the flesh when he spends his hours finding new ways to make everyone else miserable with his public brooding and obvious disappearing acts.

Take God, the Lord Jesus into your secret place where you think and devise the plans that rule your conscious hours and bury your unconscious ones. Take on that burden... the burden of telling God the truth about you in private and seeking what he would have you do in the light of day. It is the only way to finally and ultimately live without feeling like a vacation is the necessity of getting out of town and leaving yourself behind.

Where Tough Love Begins

January 30, 1994.

During the 1980s, the concept of tough love was introduced as a way of fighting back against the chaos brought upon a family by out of control adolescents. This way of handling troubled kids proposed that they needed to have the reality of individual responsibility presented to them, so that they took ownership of the consequences of their actions.

Tough love taught that love which continually went soft and let badly behaving kids off the hook, only invited more bad behavior. Real parental love was the love that taught inner discipline, which led to responsibility. This responsibility was the key to success, whereas the chaos perpetrated by permissiveness led eventually to unhappiness and failure for the misbehaving child.

As groups formed to debate this great remedy for child rearing, it became obvious to many observers that one of its great shortfalls was in the necessity of the adults to first apply to themselves the standards of responsibility. It was incongruous for a heavy smoking, alcohol-abusing parent to be "tough-loving" his child to take responsibility for his life and own the consequences of his actions, when he could not provide the role model.

In short, parents were finding that the place where tough love had to begin was in their own lives. Tough love really begins in the lives of those who apply it to themselves, if it is to be effective and be truly tough and truly love.

Jesus taught us a lot about spiritual tough love. Once a rich young man came to Jesus and asked him what more he had to do to attain eternal life. Jesus advised him to live the commandments. The young man asked, "Which ones?" Jesus answered, "The commandments of Moses, to love thy father and mother" etc. Jesus added one more to the list: to love your neighbor as yourself. The rich man replied, "I've done all of this". He then stood there waiting expectantly for Jesus to say, "Well done my young friend. You have nothing to worry about, the Kingdom is yours."

But something was lacking in the man's desire to obtain the Kingdom. It was a commitment to serve the world's pain, a commitment that flowed evenly and naturally from the love of God. This young man was willing to love God, but he was not willing to see God so passionately in the faces of those around him who were so desperately in need.

Jesus confronted the young man with the thoughtlessness of his commitment. This was an example of the spiritual tough love of Jesus Christ. When Jesus told the story of the sheep and the goats, he was also presenting to his followers and to us the visage of spiritual tough love, and like the tough love of the 80's, we discover that the place it begins is in our lives.

Jesus described an apocalyptic time when the angels judged men and women according to the worth of their lives, separating them as the shepherd separates the sheep from the goats. To some he said, "In your lives, you saw people thirsty and hungry and ill clothed and housed and you said, "I really can't feel good about living in an excess of stereo equipment and sitting around watching football while my neighbor is suffering. I'll just sell some of this stuff and do some feeding and housing and clothing of the poor; I'll give up a couple of football games and do some driving for the Deacons." Jesus taught that when you said this and did this, you said and did it to Him as well.

The rich young man knew he wanted the Kingdom in his soul. He wanted that inner radiance, power and confidence he saw in the people who followed Jesus. But he also wanted to keep a tight limit on what he did with all of the time and possessions in this life.

Just before the story of the sheep and goats, Matthew told another of the parables Jesus taught his disciples. In this story, three men were told by their master that he was going away on a business trip. He was going to leave each of them with a part of his property to take care of and invest. He made sure that the very intelligent servant was given the most to invest, the clever, but less talented man was given a bit less, and the servant who had trouble balancing his check book was given the least of all.

This was a wise plan. The servant gifted with great financial ability would have no fear of investing a great deal of money, and could keep track of all of it. The servant who had trouble balancing his checkbook was given such a small amount of the master's worth to invest, that monitoring it would not cause him much stress. As Matthew said, the Master gave each what they were capable of dealing with.

The servant with the most money went immediately to the stock market, and began to high roll on the New York Stock Exchange. Before long, he had invested his way into a rather large fortune in a diversified portfolio large enough to make even Dreyfus shut up and listen.

The second servant, knowing that he did not have the same keen sense of trading his sister had, took the master's property and invested it in mutual funds. This also created a handy return over time, since the servant invested with a wide array of funds under the guidance of an expert.

But the third servant didn't want to think about the issue of the master's property. He didn't want to risk losing anything and suffer the pain of loss, thinking that this would displease the master. Actually, what he really feared was going to the bother of doing something with what he was given. So he did nothing. He put the money in an envelope, and taped it to the underside of a desk so no one could steal it. When the master returned he gave the money back, thinking that this would at least be acceptable, since nothing had been lost.

Now, let us think about it for a moment. This servant could at least have put the money in a safe, 4% CD; all that would have taken was a quick trip to the bank. The master didn't expect him to become a financial mogul. He only wanted him to use what common sense he did have. He wanted him to walk to the bank, deposit his holdings, so they at least earned something.

The master let it be known that the committed servants were the one who risked doing something with what they were given. The two servants who had risked losing a bundle were rewarded, and the servant who never ventured out with his gift was punished. His allotment was taken away and given to the others.

This is the tough love of Jesus Christ. It is meant to be applied to our lives so that we can avoid being the third servant whose spiritual life never had enough commitment to get off of the ground. True spiritual commitment is the investing of some part of our gifts in the life of the world, for the sake of the gracious love of Jesus Christ. When we see Christ in the lives of those in pain and need, we invest ourselves in healing this pain in the way our gifts direct us.

Christian commitment isn't terribly burdensome. The servant who didn't have an aptitude for money management was not expected to become a financial genius. He wasn't given such a heavy responsibility that he could not bear it. He was given a responsibility for investing the master's wealth commensurate with his abilities. What surely bothered the master was that he didn't even do what he was clearly capable of doing.

God gives us life, security, His love and grace, our identity as His children, and varying amounts of talent. Most of us have more substance and available time than the truly poor of the earth. So the tough love of Jesus Christ asks us, what are we doing with our gifts? What is the nature of our commitment to use the gifts of God for the Glory of the Kingdom? Within the limits of our capabilities, what have we done to respond to the Christ in others who are thirsty, hurting, hungry, ill-clothed and unsheltered?

Jesus said that when the servant invested what his master gave him he received much more in return. This is the nature of true Christian commitment; it always eventuates in service. When it does not, then it is not true Christian commitment. I cannot sugar coat this wise saying from Jesus. Certainly, we can say over and over how much we love God and venerate the name and witness of Jesus Christ. However, until the image of Christ appears in the lives of others, and we are compelled by this image to invest our lives in some form of service, then we haven't really begun to live the committed Christian life.

When Christians find themselves compelled to serve, they find themselves on risky ground. It is not easy to be a servant of Jesus Christ dealing with the pain of others. People often don't react with gratitude. It is hard to know what really helps people, and what only a temporary remedy is. It is hard to know when to give assistance to people, or require that they use it to help themselves. It's usually easier just to give money to organized charities, and let someone else decide how it is to be used.

I have never found it to fail that when Christians invest their gifts in the work of the Kingdom and become servants, they always gain tremendously from what they risk. I know of no Christian servants who would wish to take back their service, regretting what they did because it didn't come out just right. What I have experienced is just what Jesus said. The servants, who are compelled by the love of God to serve according to their abilities and risk the commitment of serving, are rewarded greatly with wisdom, love, inner peace, and joy.

Spiritual tough love begins with ourselves when we take a good look at what we are doing with the gifts God has given to us. Are we hoarding them for ourselves? Are we investing them for the sake of those we love, and from whom we feel we might get a return? Have we seen Christ in the eyes of the world's want and begun to invest in filling their needs? Have we shared our talent with our Christian brothers and sisters, so we can invest corporately in the work of the Kingdom more effectively than we can as individuals?

The consequence of failing to invest our gifts in the work of the Kingdom of God is a stunted spiritual life. The consequences of investing in the Kingdom are an ever-expanded spiritual life, and a return in compound interest of the peace which passes understanding.

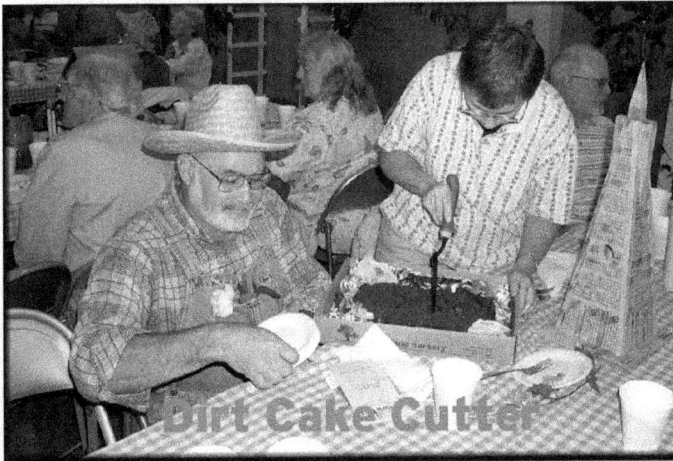

I am Farmer Bill serving cake at a stewardship event

Dressed Up With Someplace to Go

December 11, 2002

When I was in the 5th grade I took piano lessons from a wonderful woman named Mrs. Folkers. She was an expressive person who obviously loved children, and had a way of inspiring us to make music even if we were minimally inclined to do so. On one occasion she picked out a piece of music for me to learn that contained a gypsy theme, filled with minor notes, sharp notes and chords. I clunked along through the piece, making the gypsies described by the music, sound pretty weak and pathetic.

After having sat through a couple of mediocre sessions of my rendition of "Gypsy Fire," Mrs. Folkers said that the piece was able to take a lot more fire than I was giving it. I played louder, clunked harder, but to no avail. "We have a grass fire going, but we really need a forest fire," she said to me. So I asked her to play it through once like she wanted to hear it.

I scooted over to the right side of the bench, she took up the mid bench position and let her hands fly. I was electrified. The first minor grace notes set the piece rolling at lightning speed. While she lowered the volume of the sound, she didn't lower the intensity. Her musical gypsies were in your face; they were wild people filled with passion and zest, proudly stamping the ground in dance and snapping castanets. When she finished the piece I sat stunned and excited. I suddenly realized that what she had just done I was capable of doing. This was my piece of music, and with some discipline, elbow grease, and determination I could set the gypsies afire just as she had.

The human soul is like a score of music God gives to each of us to play for a lifetime. And like the my music teacher God has given us Christ to show us how much fire, and zest, and passion, and richness that score of music can contain. Like Mrs. Folkers, Jesus has demonstrated how to play the piece for maximum joy and excitement.

Louis Smedes, in *The Art of Forgiving*, gave a great example of the difference between being embarrassed about something and being caught up in false shame. He writes:

> A couple of years ago Doris (his wife) and I went to a snug, round theater called the Mark Taper Forum at the Music Center in Los Angeles to see a performance of Shakespeare's "Julius Caesar" in a modern setting. It was a matinee performance, starting at precisely 2:30 in the afternoon. It so happened that at 2:30 on that particular after noon there were exactly two minutes left to play in the deciding game of the semifinals in the NBA championship basketball playoffs. My team, the Los Angeles Lakers, was playing the Portland

Trail Blazers, and the score was tied when the curtain went up.

Looking ahead to this possibility I smuggled a Walkman inside the theater, put on the earphones, and listened to the staccato play-by-play of Chick Hern, the Lakers' broadcaster, while I watched the first scene of the tragedy of Julius Caesar unfold.

My wife glanced at me; I thought she was asking me to tell her the score of the basketball game. I intended to whisper it for only her ears to hear, but the crowd at the basketball game was yelling and screaming in my earphones and I had to make myself heard above the racket, which I did. I yelled, "Eighteen seconds to go; Lakers down by a point!"

Fifteen rows ahead of me, startled patrons turned around, shocked. Mark Antony missed a cue.

At intermission time I needed to find a bathroom, and I decided to make my move out into the lobby. A tike of a woman half my size and more than my age was waiting for me; she blocked my path and hissed that I ought to be ashamed of myself. I told her I was sorry and that it was an accident. No excuse; she just hoped to God my shameful behavior was a momentary lapse and not a way of life and that I ought to be ashamed and stand up and apologize to the cast. People standing around in the lobby listened to her and watched me; they were on her side.

For three days, I felt like a fatally flawed person standing shamed before the harsh judgment of my cultured superiors. But was it shame...Or acute chagrin? For a little while, I suffered shame for being an inferior human being, and then, brought back to sanity, I felt embarrassment at being a nincompoop at the theater.

Louis Smedes remembered what his teacher had said about the music his soul could make. Christ has rescued us from that grinding doubt that we are worthy at the core.

So when people or circumstances want to muffle our soul's music with this kind of undeserved shame, we need to disallow it, and ignore it, and continue to make the music Christ directs us to play.

Jane and I are dressed with many places to go

Choosing Life

March 12, 2000

Deuteronomy 30: 11-20

Mark 1:9-11

When the remnant population of Israel came out of captivity in Chaldea in the 6th century B.C.E., they desperately sought to rally themselves into a significant society once again. They looked to their faith leaders to give them a way to live which would not again find them as fragmented as they had been when they tried to utter the name of Yahweh on the banks of the Tigris rather than on the shores of the Jordan. So it was that the Divines of that day sought the counsel of God, and coupling this inspiration with their best wisdom they took up the old book of Deuteronomy and expanded it to include our passage from Chapter 30. The corpus of the old book had been found in the temple in Jerusalem during the reign of Josiah in 621 B.C.E. Its discovery had begun a revolution of religious devotion. And the priests who carefully expanded the book in the 6th Century hoped that their devoted work would rekindle the fires of faith as much as the reading of the older book had done.

The priests discerned that what God asked of all of them was a fundamental examination of the basic choices by which they would lead their lives. God sought from his people in that day a choice between life and death as a people and a civilization. God wanted them to choose a spiritual life and reject a life of spiritual emptiness. So those immortal words were penned into the 30th chapter of Deuteronomy:

> I call heaven and earth to witness against you this day: that I have set before you life and death, blessing and curse; therefore choose life that you and your descendants may live...
>
> *Deuteronomy 30:19*

When Jesus was baptized in the Jordan by John the Baptist, he was affirmed as the promised anointed one who would bring salvation to his nation and all people. After this, the text tells us, the Spirit drove Jesus out into the desert where he was beset by the demons of temptation. For 40 days he lived there, fasting, praying obviously wrestling with his own human nature and purifying what was needed in order to really do what he was required to do in order to make meaningful choices and fulfill his destiny.

We read this text on the first Sunday of Lent because this order of events in Jesus' life has created a time-tested tradition in the Christian faith. It is a tradition of regularly examining the choices by which we live our lives. Like Jesus, we do not do this before we are baptized, but afterwards. We do it so that, like Jesus, we can be clear about what we are doing to fulfill a destiny, which strengthens the Kingdom of God.

So during these next 40 days of Lent we will be using the Sunday reflection time to examine the great choices set before us which are the choices of spiritual life and death of our day and age. What I am suggesting that we do in these next few Sundays is hold all of our major choices up against the level of the witness of Christ to see if they are out of plumb.

In Herman Melville's immortal story, *Moby Dick*, he describes a lamp, which hung in the captain's cabin aboard the *"Pequod."* He wrote that no matter which way the ship yawed or pitched in the waves, the lantern hung exactly perpendicular, as he says, "revealing the false, and lying level of everything else."

I'm suggesting that we see how much of what we have already chosen and how what we have before us to choose is level or out of plumb with the compassionate grace, justice and mercy of Christ.

For like Jesus we too have the demons of tempting choices seeking to derail our resolve to live real Christian's lives.

The March, 2000 issue of *Homiletics* tells of this story of a man who lived in a Mexican village and made his living fishing. An American businessman was at the pier of the coastal Mexican village when the man pulled up in his small boat and tied up. Inside the small I boat were several large yellow fin tuna. The American complimented the man on the quality of his fish and asked how long it took to catch them. The fisherman replied only a little while.

The American then asked why didn't he stay out longer and catch more fish. The fisherman said he had enough to support his family's immediate needs. The American then asked, "But what do you do with the rest of your time?" The fisherman said, "I sleep late, fish a little; play with my children, take siesta with my wife, Maria, stroll into the village each evening where I sip wine and play guitar with my amigos. I have a full and busy life, senor."

The American scoffed,

> I am a Harvard MBA and could help you. You should spend more time fishing; and with the proceeds, buy a bigger boat, and with the proceeds from the bigger boat, you could buy several boats; eventually you would have fleet of fishing boats. Instead of selling your catch to a middleman, you would sell directly to the processor, eventually opening your own cannery. You would control the product, processing and distribution. You would need to leave this small coastal fishing village and move to Mexico City, then LA and eventually NYC where you will run your expanding enterprise.

The Mexican fisherman asked, "But Senor, how long will this all take?"

To which the American replied, "Fifteen to twenty years."

"But what then, Senor?"

The American laughed and said, "That's the best part. When the time is right, you would announce an IPO and sell your company stock to the public and become very rich; you would make millions."

"Millions, Senor?" Then what...?"

The American said, "Then you would retire. Move to a small coastal fishing village where you would sleep late, fish a little, play with your kids, take siesta with your wife, stroll to the village in the evenings where you could sip wine and play your guitar with your amigos."

If you look at a road map of California it is clear that in order to get to the Sierras on foot there are many routes an individual can take. Some will be more direct than others, but there are many variations, especially if the goal is just to arrive at any point as long as it is somewhere on this mountain chain. But if one starts on foot and heads west, it is clear that the Sierras will never appear before the walker drowns in the Pacific. Generally what we know is that one should head in an easterly course as opposed to a westerly direction. But once headed east, there are many choices, which can keep one going east.

So it is with God. I do not think that we have one special destiny, which we are to discern out of the mind of God. But I do believe, as does the witness of our scriptures, that there are several choices that lead to destinies headed for the light of God. Just so, there are many choices, which lead to destinies headed west and into a drowning in a life of self-absorption, materialism, negativity, and empty living, which lead away from God.

Woe to the person who tries to set the destiny of faith of another. Could the businessman in our story really have the best interests of the soul of the fisherman in mind by suggesting the destiny he himself found fulfilling? In fact, just as the businessman questioned the direction of the fisherman, so equally the fisherman could have questioned the choices of the businessman.

There is a cute story about a young mother who saw her daughter sitting and playing with a plethora of educational toys she had purchased in order to stimulate her daughter to robust thoughts about the future. She felt a rush of satisfaction as she watched her daughter finger the abacus and build patterns with it. And a particular swell of pride came over her when her daughter picked up the stethoscope and placed the receivers in her ears. Placing the sensor first against her chest, the little girl then placed it against her mouth and to her mother's dismay she said quite plainly and maturely, "Welcome to McDonalds, May I take your order?"

So the question of choices begins with us this Lenten season, just after we have taken the Sacraments and promised anew to infuse our lives with the love and joy of Christ, and to be a taste of the Sacrament to the world around us. In light of this sacrament, what is the nature of the choices you have made up to this point in your life? Remember that we are looking at these choices through the eyes of Jesus, who isn't shocked by our errors and our misdeeds. Jesus isn't out to slam dunk us, or to run us out of town on a rail. Jesus is with us to help us steer east instead of west, along a myriad of choices which all lead to fulfillment of God.

Have you chosen life? Have your life choices put you in a pretty good position to be loving, caring, compassionate, generous, forgiving, joyful in what you have, unobsessed by what you don't have? Do you have plans for a future? Do they include the things of God, or are you waiting until everything is secure and then you'll think about things like benevolence, time with those you say you love, time for self understanding, discernment of where God really moves in your life? The text of today suggests that this set of priorities may be a way to slide into a drift west instead of east. Use Lent to check it out.

Once, a Roman soldier approached Jesus, begging him to heal his servant. Jesus said he would go to his home and do so, but the soldier demurred. He was embarrassed to have Jesus see his quarters, and he believed in Jesus so much that he said, "You have only to order it and my servant will be healed." Jesus told this man that he was traveling in the right direction to hit the Kingdom. His loving concern for his servant, his tender caring for him and his great faith in Jesus' power to heal were signs of the choices he was making which were heading him east instead of west.

An educated young man whose parents had made sure he saw all of the right schools and sat with all the right and notable religious scholars of the day felt something was missing from his life. So he asked Jesus just what he had to do to be assured that he was heading east toward God instead of West and gradually away from God. Jesus told him. Sell what you have and follow me.

Get unwound from your wealth, and learn some humility then you'll be sure of going east. But he couldn't face that choice and didn't want to understand it. So he wandered off, wondering why he felt he heard the sea pounding the shore just over the horizon ahead of him.

Lent is a time to make examine choices. It is a time to choose life, to head east to see the world from the mountaintops, and to clearly mark the choices, which will lead you to an epiphany or a spiritual drowning.

Rejoice there are many roads leading east. And God waits at the end of every one of them. Enjoy your journey.

Spiritual Detox

July 15, 2001

Colossians 3:1-17

In Paul's letter to the church in the city of Colossae he wrote that those who believed in Christ should have a new character. This character would be rid of the negative and self-destructive outcomes of inner-passions. So, Paul wrote,

> But now you must get rid of all such things, anger, wrath, malice, slander, and abusive language from your mouth. Do not lie to one another, seeing that you have stripped off the old self with its practices and have clothed yourselves with the new self, which is being renewed in knowledge according to the image of its creator.
>
> *Colossians 3:8-10*

Paul tells us to renew ourselves in knowledge according to the image of our creator. This means that as people of faith we can and should constantly bring before God's grace and loving power, the toxic parts of our lives. Paul says:

> As God's chosen ones, holy and beloved, clothe yourselves with compassion, kindness, humility, meekness, and patience. Bear with one another and, if anyone has a complaint against another,

forgive each other...clothe yourselves with love, which binds everything together in perfect harmony. Let the peace of Christ rule in your hearts, and be thankful.

Colossians 3:12-15

There are many spiritual toxins, which need the love and grace of God in order to lose their potency in our lives. When a person enters alcoholics anonymous and begins the process of detoxification, he or she is lead to sobriety through a 12-step Program. This program requires that the person first admit his powerlessness over alcohol, that is, admit he is an alcoholic. Secondly the person states that he has come to believe that a power greater than himself can restore his sobriety and third, that he will turn his will over to the power of God.

But in order to really unhitch himself from the power of the drug he has to dig further into the moral and spiritual toxins which lay behind his dependence on the drugs. In step four the person must make a fearless moral inventory of his life, pinpointing the toxic patterns poisoning his ability to cope with life. In step five he is asked to admit to God and at least one other human being the exact nature of the places where he has done wrong and allowed these toxins to become harmful to himself and others.

The next step is for him to be entirely ready for God to remove these toxic parts of his character. Then he must ask God's help to do so.

These first seven steps are part of the most successful program I know that unhitches people from one of the greatest scourges of our society. The power of this program says something to those of us who aren't struggling with alcohol addiction, but are struggling with many of the same spiritual and moral toxins, which appear when we take a personal moral and spiritual inventory.

In Robert Schuller's book *Turning Hurts into Halos*, Dr. Schuller gives a checklist of negative reactions which poison the ability of a person to accept help. He lists some of the major toxins which must be eliminated if we are to be able to live a renewed life by the power of our Creator.

We begin the list with anger. This is at the top of Dr. Schuller's list and he says simply, "Dump your anger. It will destroy you. Get rid of this emotional enemy."

I realize that many will argue that we must maintain certain anger, such as the outrage over the holocaust, or the senseless extermination of 3 million Cambodians by the Pol Pot government. But I must on the whole concur with Dr. Schuller. Keeping your anger over past hurts drains your life of the energy that could be directed to give hope, or love, or creativity, or a host of other positive, peace producing activities.

During the great protest years of the 1960s and thereafter, it was popular to intone the cause of righteous anger over the wrongs of the world. People felt justified in taking bold steps, even destructive steps righting these wrongs. All too often individuals quietly fed into this moral outrage the personal anger they felt over negative past experiences and hurtful memories as far back as their early childhood. Soon the controlled burn of anger at social injustice became a raging inferno of indignation, which resisted the power of reason or love to cool it down. In actuality the fire of personal anger was nurtured and kept burning by the fuel of the social cause.

Examine your anger carefully. As you prayerfully meditate before the loving and forgiving presence of God, ask yourself how much of your anger is really worth preserving and how much simply needs to be hosed down with love and buried with humor and new hope. Then do it.

Guilt is another toxin which poisons our ability to live in the image of God. Some of us live with guilt over some specific act we have done or left undone which has harmed others. In these cases Christian faith urges people to do as the 12-step Program recommends. Face the fact that God lovingly invites you to bring this act before him and sort it out. Where it is possible without causing greater harm to others, make amends for the wrongful act, offer apologies, and know that God forgives and you are secure in God's love.

One of the most common expressions of guilt is the general feeling that one is living a lie; the nagging thought that if people really knew the kind of person I really am they would know I'm not as smart as they think, or strong as they think, or as good as they think.

The apostle Peter was a victim of this kind of free-floating guilt. When Jesus stood in the boat and revealed himself to be filled with holiness, Peter was smitten with this guilt and fell to his knees before Jesus saying, "Go away from me Lord, for I am a sinful man."

Jesus said to him, "Peter don't be afraid." He was letting Peter know he was just the sort of fellow he had been looking for; one of those people who feel deep down that he's not really worthy. He wanted Peter to know that none of that mattered to him or to God, and as Peter fully realized that truth, he would convince others that God really loves them too despite all this "guilt."

If you're like Peter, falling to your knees in guilt, remember what Jesus did with all that guilt. He simply dumped it over the rail and took Peter into the fold. Do likewise.

Schuler lists destructive pride as the third toxin that keeps one from being a whole person in Christ. Destructive pride appears when healthy self-esteem becomes too egotistical, or too driven by insecurities. Destructive pride hates to admit mistakes; it tries to tear others down in order to keep itself inflated.

Destructive pride can't just forgive and forget. It has to save face, restore its place, or just get even. At its worse, it forgets who God is and becomes like the character in Clarence Day's book, *Life with Father*. Day writes, "Father expected a good deal of God. He didn't actually accuse God of inefficiency, but when he prayed his tone was lucid and angry-- like that of a dissatisfied guest in a carelessly managed hotel."

Is your pride hurting you and others? Then it's the wrong stuff, not the right stuff. Sort it out in prayer and meditation. God isn't afraid of what you've done with your false pride. The Lord will help you realize your misdirected reactions and find contentment in the grace of God.

The fear of embarrassment is a toxin, which keeps many of us from truly approaching the table of opportunity God has set before us in life.

When I was in seminary I worked as a custodian at a local grammar school which opened its auditorium to city sponsored adult programs in the evening. One of these programs was a dancing class. So night after night I was charged with opening and closing the facility and simply waiting around, reading a book until the program was finished. Night after night I watched as women dragged reluctant men to the dance floor. I could tell by watching these men that they really were interested in learning to dance, but they were constrained by the terrible embarrassment over appearing silly, or stupid. Little by little, over the course of time, the very patient instructor coaxed these men out of their embarrassment, and they were soon dancing, enjoying themselves as never before. By the time the program was over it appeared to me that the men had been finally let out of a self-imposed prison ... the prison of the fear of embarrassment.

God has given us value. It cost God a great price in the crucifixion of His Son. Why eclipse this value with unfounded fears of embarrassment? Enjoy the process of living as the gifted human God created you to be and shine without untoward fears of embarrassment.

The fear of failure has to rank equally with the fear of embarrassment for its power to poison our ability to live in God's image. I am always amazed by the number of really brilliant people I know who will not allow themselves to participate in enjoyable experiences because they are afraid that they will appear as failures.

So it is that an interest in painting, investing, trying another job, playing word games with the family, water skiing with friends, or other activities, is stifled just because of the fear of failing.

The worst thing about this fear is that it prevents us from pursuing the normal path to success, a path that can wind it way through failures. R.H. Macy failed seven times before his store in New York caught on. Babe Ruth struck out 1,330 times, but he also hit 714 home runs. Even when failure is not followed by great success, the information and experience it brings is always valuable as it is applied to our lives.

The fear of success is another toxin that stifles our lives and hopes. It is born of the thought that if we succeed we are going to have to maintain the aura of being worthy of our success. This is a real fear that gnaws at us when things are starting to turn out well, and in our fear we often sabotage ourselves.

If we understand our value to God, we will not fear failure. We equally will not expect unending success. We will know that in life and in death we belong to God, so certainly in success and in failure, God will sustain us.

To these toxins I would also add perfectionism. There is great value in doing things well, but sometimes it is driven by something a little darker and crazier. It is laced with the need to control too much. It is tinted with the fear of failure and perhaps laced with some egotism gone to seed. At any rate, perfectionism can keep one from the table of grace where good enough is the order of the day. It is a toxin when it creates unnecessary rifts between people, and brings about unnecessary anxieties. It needs the spotlight of the grace of God, who shows mercy to our shortcomings, and says to people like Peter that their imperfect lives are good enough to join the company of Christ.

I invite you to review your own lives and ask which toxins are at work in your life. Perhaps there are important toxins I haven't mentioned here which are poisoning your ability to live in the image of God.

Whatever you find in your search for toxins, I encourage you to set about today to detox your life with the antidotes of prayer and meditation, letting yourself be in the restoring presence of God's grace. Spend a good deal of time praising and giving thanks to God for all the great things in the life around you, and be sure to include the good things in yourself. The toxins can be washed away by the acceptance of the wonderful things God has given to us in the life, death and resurrection of Christ.

In my seminary days, I worked as a youth leader. On a mission trip to Mexico, we were moving rocks in 113° heat.

Cougars in the Hills

November 10, 1996

Did you know that there are cougars in the hills around town? It's true, at least one cougar. Last week when I told Phil George the title of the sermon "Cougars in the Hills" so he could put it on the sign out front he told me that he had seen a cougar in the hills behind the Veteran's hospital. It was a big one he said.

When I told this to Dennis Keller, music director, Dennis said any cougar he would see running free and near him would be a big one. These reports can be 'fear-producing' can't they? The media reported not long ago the separate stories of female joggers, who were out running alone and were attacked and killed by these big cats.

When some of the junior high students of our Presbyterian Camp Westminster Woods were hiking in the hills near the camp last summer, they found the tracks of a large cat.. a cougar. The sense of fear spread like wildfire among the kids. The Forest Service was alerted and asked its advice. It said laconically, you had over 100 Junior Highs out there in the hills, and it takes only about 20 Junior Highs to scare a cougar or anything else out of the area. Don't worry.

But I suppose some will worry and will never send their kids back to the camp again. Perhaps napalming the forest flat and shooting everything that moves would calm such fears, but even then I'm not sure. We live in a time when our media casts a fog of fears around us and many of us frantically seek complete safety and security that can never exist and is unhealthy to our spiritual lives.... as well as being kind of boring.

If we're not careful we could end up like the farmer who was visited by a stranger. The stranger came by one day in July when the farmer was sitting in front of his shack just looking around. The stranger asked, "How's your cotton coming?"

"Ain't got none" was the answer. "Didn't plant none ...afraid of the boll weevil."

"Well, how's your corn?"

"Didn't plant none...afraid of the drought.

"How about your potatoes?"

"Ain't got none... scared of tater bugs."

The stranger finally asked, "Well, what did you plant?"

"Nothin," answered the farmer. "I just played it safe."

In the Bible God is always leading fearful people to overcome their fear of losing safety and security. In this process, even when the fear is not totally mastered they realize the identity that God has coded into their genes and life experiences. Moses, the man who spoke with a stammer, finally pleaded with God to just please send someone else, but God wouldn't hear it. And of his fear, came the great, humble leader of the Exodus. Mary was called as a teenager to be the mother of Christ. Deborah was raised up in a culture negative to the leadership of a woman to be the Judge of 12th Century tribal Israel. Peter was sure he did not have the aptitude to be a disciple, and told Jesus that he was a man of unclean lips, unfit to even be in his presence. And Jesus said, "What wonderful fear, and how aware of it you are... a perfect situation for one who would follow me and be fisherman of human souls."

Even Jesus had to confront his fear in Gethsemane when in his final moments before the revelation of his betrayal he sat in the Garden after dinner alone and asked God to remove the cup of suffering he saw awaiting him. Gethsemane is the place where Jesus examined the content of human fear ... and it was there that the resolve to go to the cross rather than give in was born.

Our fears are full of content. They are sermons to our souls of some of the best work we can do to bring significance, joy, courage, strength to our lives. Hearing their content and acting upon their message does not mean that all fears will go away, although I believe most will significantly diminish.

Our more personal fears have even greater lessons for us and hold greater rewards when examined in the light of God's love. Some of us fear personal failures. Behind these fears is often a notion that we have only so much worth. And if we keep losing it by personal daily "failures", we will soon be worth little or nothing. So we want to win arguments, because losing is failure. We want to win points. We do not want to participate in activities that may be fun, educational, connectional to our loves, because we will fail to look good, do well, be graceful, or look like we have expert potential. So we starve ourselves of many experiences, many connections, because we will not participate, will not say we are sorry, admit that we are really wrong, will not join discussion of topics in which we cannot shine.

We fear intimacy.

We fear authority.

We fear the world's violence.

We fear loneliness.

We fear giving up prejudices about things.

Each of these fears contains great truths about us, truths which when lay before the graciousness of God in prayer and contemplation, will give us much greater wisdom, and courage.

In his book, *Illustrations Unlimited*, James Hewitt relates a story he heard somewhere: Once in the dead of a rainy night in the country, a man who was traveling to a conference between large cites had a blowout. When he opened his car trunk he discovered that he had a jack but to his chagrin he had no lug wrench--the gizmo that takes off the bolts that hold on the wheel. The light from a farmhouse could be seen from the road so he set out on foot through the driving rain.

At first he thought to himself that the farmer would surely have lug wrench. Then he thought that the farmer would be asleep in his warm dry bed and maybe wouldn't answer the door. If he did, he thought he would be pretty angry at being awakened in the dead night. The man's shoes were filled with water and he was beginning to shiver. He could see it in his head. The farmer would get up, bang around angrily and yell "What's the big idea waking me up at this hour?" He was always afraid of imposing on people, and this was really imposing. He was sure it would be taken that way. The fear of having to impose and be yelled at began to make him mad.

What right did the farmer have to just leave him shivering in the rain? Only a selfish clod would do that. Couldn't he see that he had to impose?

So when he got to the house he banged loudly on the door. A light went on and a voice called out "Who is it?"

His face white with anger, the soaked traveler who feared imposing called out, "You know darn well who it is. It's me. And you can keep your blasted lug wrench. I wouldn't borrow it now if you had the last one earth."

The good news is not really the Good News about security that removes our fears; so much as it is Good News about courage that allows us to face our fears.

Three Months in England

September 19, 1982

Luke 11:1-13

It's interesting how a book or passages of scripture seem to come to mind after we experience something that brings the truth of the written word to our attention.

Chapter 11 from the book of Luke and Dave Jacobson's book *Clarity in Prayer* would have been great help to my experience in England had I read and pondered them both in depth before boarding TWA flight 760.

My trip to England was not supposed to be a vacation of three months. I had agreed to vacation in England and Europe for one month and work in the London Street United Reformed Church in Basingstoke for two months. As I surveyed the definition of 'work' under these conditions, I felt that the work would be so exciting and pleasurable that the whole three months would seem like a vacation.

The long plane ride and resulting jet lag were ominous signs of tensions to come.

Those of you who have traveled with small children realize how grueling these conditions can be. We arrived tired and disoriented. The children were obviously impressed with the fact that: they were a very long way away from home, friends and anything familiar; living where people spoke with strange accents; unlikely to go home to anything familiar and secure for a very long time; and living with an increasingly uptight father.

As soon as I heard people speaking in those wonderfully correct British tones, everything incorrect about my very being seemed to come into focus. I found myself speaking slower, more grammatically. And most of all, I found myself yearning for my son of two (almost three) years to greet our new friends with proper behavioral syntax.

Luckily for us, our first encounter with England's family life came from our friends the Harrises, members of the Basingstoke Church who, along with the Marions here in Livermore, had put together the pastoral exchange.

My son responded to his new environment with growing irritability, but the Harrises graciously accepted and bid me to do the same and await his adjustment. I heard their wisdom with my head. Hearing it with my heart and soul was a number of weeks and hardships away.

I told people, as an excuse for my son's wild behavior, that he was off his pins; or so it seemed to me. When we were introduced to the congregation at Basingstoke for the first time, we were asked to come forward as a family, stand on the central platform, framed picturesquely by the large cross in the center apse.

I must tell you first off, Southern English folk are reserved. The kind of rapid response Americans give a pastor is not a tradition in southern England, especially where a reserved measured response to life is valued. Penetrating the cultural reserve was a job I hadn't really thought much about. When my son fell to the floor kicking and screaming in protest, it was clear that he was breaking one of the rules - the rule that says noisy, boisterous children need to be restrained and taught manners. I looked to the congregation for some flicker of understanding of our plight, as I knew there would have been at our home church.

Margaret Corrich Smith, the church secretary, simply plowed on in warm formality, expressing a welcome to us, raising her voice to overcome the rising pitch of my son who was at that point, trying to bite the rug.

When my wife initially brought the children into church that morning, with all eyes glued to her back, Chris had done the same thing in the aisle. She said that for an instant she thought of flinging herself on the floor beside him, along with my daughter, hoping everyone would think this prostration was some strange devotional act of Californians.

I was less creative. I was furious at Chris and I wanted nothing less than to throttle him. Judging from the way he was going about his hysterics, it was clear that manhandling him would leave me red-faced, panting with anger and fluttering about in the pastor's borrowed ill-fitting robe. I tried to smile knowingly at the congregation, and at the same time, glare meaningfully at Chris.

That was the beginning of my question to God and me - what's happening to my son here? And what can I do to change his disturbing behavior.

We decided that what the kids needed to get acquainted with England was a play school experience. So we took them to the churche's play school. I watched my son gloomily eye the prospects about him that first day, and then make his way to an English boy of his own age and size. I was delighted - at first. But horrified, when without a word, Christopher drew back his arm and decked his potential companion with an uncoordinated, but effective right cross.

We all, of course, flapped about. The teacher smiled and said in typical English understatement - "A bit enthusiastic isn't he?"

I was again furious with Chris. Furious and determined to stop this upsetting behavior which was embarrassing his parents and, I thought, alienating so many in this more disciplined and reserved congregation.

I finally decided to do something drastic. I shut myself up alone early one morning and I prayed. I decided to say exactly what I felt, ask for exactly what I wanted and then just try to listen to see what came back.

My prayer came out as a muddled mass of tangled requests. I felt like I had gone to seek God's peace in prayer and instead I was sitting there in the early morning, stuttering at the feet of God.

Dave Jacobson in his book on prayer, counsels that when we pray we ought to make sure we ask for what we want in specific and honest terms. He points out that in doing so, we begin to define what it is that we are really seeking, and often that is a far cry from what we started out asking for.

I asked specifically for some way to quell my son's boisterousness so that I wouldn't be embarrassed by him amid my "reserved" parishioners. I prayed to prevent my son's outbreaks of anger; to suppress them so that I wouldn't be seen as a lax parent who didn't know how to control his own son.

The next time I prayed I had to ask for some way to separate my concern for my son's behavior from my own concern for the way people saw me as pastor and parent. I had to admit that I couldn't seem to make the separation, which had resulted in my overblown, impatient anger!

It seemed like the more honest and persistent and personal that I became in my prayers, the more the problem changed, the more I changed.

Luke 11 bids us to pray continually, persistently. It doesn't ask us to pray that way because God doesn't hear us the first time. It asks us to pray that way so that we become aware of what exactly we are asking for and then exactly what God is doing about it.

The more I delved in prayer, into asking about what was happening with my son, the more I discovered about my own motivation, my own part of the problem and my own power in working a solution.

I wanted a quick fix to a very large problem. I had taken a 2-year-old away from his home, friends, and security. I had taken him to a strange place where his father was continually preoccupied with feelings of which he had to be careful, be proper, and be agreeable to win the respect and love of his English congregation.

The more I prayed honestly about my son, the more I came to understand what I really was asking, what was really possible, and what I really needed to ask. At first, I did what Dave Jacobson counsels us not to do in prayer - I censored my prayer. Instead of pouring out every bit of anguish and doubt about the situation, I prayed something benign like, "O.K. Lord, help me to know how to quell my son's restless spirit, give me the tools to cool his anger and temper his outbursts."

Jacobson tells us there are three ways prayer is answered. The answers to prayer usually come when our honest petitioning finally focuses our attention on what we really mean to ask for, and openly asks God to help us get what we really need.

Prayer is answered, Dave writes, through a change in attitude or state of mind. It is answered by gaining peace of mind or a quieter heart. And it may be answered with a change in physical experience.

My own was answered in the first two ways. I realize that the change in the third depends some on how much I keep the other two ways alive and well.

I began praying uncensored, honest and hopeful prayers, seeking, probing and stuttering. I ended being granted the peace of the Holy Spirit.

I no longer ask for ways to control Chris; but now I seek to understand better what my reactions to him mean, and how to communicate to him what my deepest love of him intends. The seeking goes on in my prayer life and the answers keep coming.

Are we praying as Jesus taught, continually, seeking, honestly, listening, asking, and defining as we lay our petitions at the feet of God?

I discovered the help such praying offers during my three months in England. I commend to you Jesus' words, "For everyone who asks, receives, and he who seeks, finds, and to him who knocks, it will be opened."

Jean and me with our family in England

The Eyes of the Heart (Excerpts)

January 21, 1996

Excerpt #1

In *Nouns and Adverbs*, Cyrus Augustus relates that several years ago a teacher assigned to visit children in a large city hospital received a routine call requesting that she visit a particular child. She took the boy's name and room number and was told by the teacher on the other end of the line, "We're studying nouns and adverbs in his class now. I'd be grateful if you could help him with his homework so he doesn't fall behind the other students."

It wasn't until the visiting teacher arrived at the boy's room, that she realized it was located in the hospital's burn unit. No one had prepared her to find a young boy, horribly burned and in great pain. She felt that she couldn't just turn and walk out, so she awkwardly stammered, "I'm the hospital teacher and your teacher sent me to help you with nouns and adverbs."

The next morning a nurse on the burn unit asked her, "What did you do to that boy?" Before she could finish a profusion of apologies, the nurse interrupted her; "You don't understand. We've been very worried about him, but ever since you were here yesterday, his whole attitude has changed. He's fighting back, responding to treatment. It's as though he's decided to live."

The boy later explained that he had completely given up hope until the teacher came into his room. Everything changed when he came to a simple realization: With joyful tears he expressed it this way: "They wouldn't send a teacher to a dying boy to work on nouns and adverbs, would they?

Paul said that God would not send Himself to us in Christ, if we were worthless. The eyes of the heart enlightened by the love of Christ see the world with HOPE - hope which is as powerful as the hope that made that little boy change his attitude toward his terrible injuries. And that hope is transmittable to others in the way we give out the Good News of Christ, in our choosing, our loving and sharing~

Excerpt #2

When my foster father became afflicted with Alzheimer's, I came to know my foster mother better. During that wonderful, but tragic time we had together, she and I had to visit a local automobile body shop to see about getting a fender repaired after a young man had run a red light and crashed into her car. The man at the body shop took one look at my mom and saw a frail, elderly woman, living on bottled oxygen and without a great amount of formal education.

He raised his voice and let her know that he was going to take care of her really well.

He wanted her to know how the world of terrible people worked; how my mom would be left holding the bag if she didn't do some clever maneuvering in her handling of the accident. The man looked at the way my mom sat there silently, her mouth shut tightly, looking at him with her brow troubled, and thinking that he had her undivided attention. He told her she should visit his lawyer and his doctor, who would fit her with a neck collar for the little twinge of pain she might have from the accident. And his lawyer would fix her up with a legal interpretation of her accident that would not only fix her fender, but her bank account as well.

I looked at my mom and saw a strong, God fearing, farm girl, who had walked 78 years upon the earth, cared for two grown children and 319 foster children. She had lived through a grinding economic depression, and sent her husband off to war. She was a woman who refused to believe that hucksters knew more about the world, because they chose to see all of its rubbish and moral poverty. Her knitted brow was the sign of a determination to resist a temptation she considered a silly sin, and a concern that this young man was so out of touch with his soul, that he would blatantly suggest that she lie for money.

When she got up and said, "Thanks for the information," and headed for the door, the young man couldn't believe that she was turning him down and walking out. But she did. Too bad the eyes of his heart were not made clear by the light of Christ, so that he could have seen the richness that dwelled in the heart of my mother. It was the richness that easily turned aside the temptation to cheat. It was the richness I was blessed to see so clearly, in those last years we had together.

When we see with the eyes of the heart, enlightened by the Spirit of the love of Christ and the grace of God, we see the immeasurable power of God's love everywhere.

A Programmed Encounter

December 27, 1981

If we are to fully grasp the significance of the Christmas season, we need to spend some time in quiet reflection. This is probably hard for many of us during all of the hustle and bustle of gift purchasing, holiday parties, working, or if you're not employed, feeling even lower than usual when personal finances are not up to expectations.

It seems the Christmas sales pitches now begin inordinately early. Apparently, the fear of retailers that the economy may be slowing down, impels them to lure us into the marketplace at every opportunity. So it is no wonder that finding this quiet, reflective time is so hard to do.

After the season is over, we need to keep alive the quiet, meaningful part of Christmas for another day. We must come away from this season with its significance spiritually renewed for our use, in what could be another year of challenges and difficulties.

Poet W. H. Auden wrote about the spiritual meaning of the birth of Jesus Christ. In his poem, *After Christmas,* he said that for him, reflection upon this great event that so changed the course of human history is like entering an experience where, for once in his life, "everything" became a "you" and nothing was an "it".

He then points out something that has become, for me, especially characteristic of our fast paced, computerized time. He said that having experienced this feeling of everything being a "you" and nothing being an "it" at the stable of the new born Christ, we crave the sensation, but ignore the cause.

Ravi Shankar, the great Indian sitar player and music composer, became the toast of the American popular music scene when he introduced his skill into its genre. Pop composers crowded round to learn how to make this instrument sing and reproduce its spiritual effects on those who heard it.

Shankar found out what Auden said about the human drive for spirituality. He discovered that these American students often didn't care that his music was clothed in much prayer and spiritual reflection upon life, God, the soul, human destiny, and the spiritual sources of human peace. Too many of these enthusiasts only wanted to reproduce the sensations they had while hearing the music and ignore the cause.

Ravi Shankar, if you will remember, at one time became incensed at these responses and angrily withdrew back to his native India. As he did, he exclaimed that he would not teach sitar apart from what made the soul respond to its voice.

The cause of our light says the book of John, is the advent of God's spirit into human flesh and the witness of that person to all who hear his words, perceive his meaning, and align themselves with His Word Way.

We cannot walk in the light by simply reveling in a few mindless, uncommitted experiences with it. We cannot claim discipleship simply because we find that we are inspired to emotional highs by candles, beautiful stories, and sacred music. Nor can we understand why Ravi Shankar believes in God just because we like his music. It is possible to experience God and then ignore the cause; but to do so throughout a lifetime is to deprive our souls of what I John calls—"A walk in the light."

> If then we say that we have fellowship with him, yet at the same time live in the darkness, we are lying both in our words and in our actions. But if we live in the light--just as he is in the light--then we have fellowship with one another, and the blood of Jesus, his Son purifies us from every sin.

I John 1:6-7

William Barclay, in *New Testament Studies* explains, John is writing to counteract one heretical and mistaken way of thought. There were those who claimed to be especially intellectually and spiritually advanced, but whose lives showed no sign of that. They claimed to have progressed so far along the road of knowledge that, for them, sin ceased to matter.

They claimed to be so spiritual that sin was of no account at all. They claimed to be so far ahead, the lows ceased to exist. It is on record that Napoleon once said that lows were made for ordinary people, but were never meant for the likes of him.

So these heretics claimed to be so far along that even if they did sin, it was of no importance whatsoever.

In later days Clement of Alexandria tells us that there were heretics who said that it makes no difference how a man lives. They said that nothing brought any risk to a really spiritual man. Irenaus tells us that they declared that a truly spiritual man was quite incapable of ever incurring any pollution or infection, no matter what kind of deeds he did. These people in effect said that they had risen to a height in which sin did not matter."

This obviously bothered John a great deal. So he writes clearly his belief that one cannot live in the light and have no effects of what the light illuminates in his own life. Indeed, for John, when one lives in God's light, and takes seriously the cause of the good experience at Christmas, one finds a new world out there. And having found a new world, he acts differently than he once did.

Because a person has seen the landscape lit up by a burst of light, it does not mean that the person will be able to walk a straight and productive path when the light goes away. We don't remember enough in those short bursts of light, nor really see enough, to set a course through the landscape without corrections for dangerous obstacles and pitfalls.

A friend of mine was once led on a hiking expedition by a friend of his who claimed to know every detail of the landscape they were to traverse. So, when it became too dark to hike, the friend "guide" insisted they plunge on to his favorite spot, where waking up in the morning would be spectacularly glorious. So they plodded on, groping in the little daylight that was left. They had to practically crawl into their sleeping positions when the guide finally declared the paradisiacal spot was gained, aided only by the dim rays from small pocket lights. Morning came; and the early light showed the campers exquisite beauty, but it also showed the shocked guide about 2,000 other campers lodged in every nook and cranny all around them. The beauty the guide had remembered had been so wrapped in solitude that the truth of daylight displayed a different scene.

John says that to live in the Spirit, to live being inspired by the Christmas event, we must continually turn its light on to what is before us. As we do that, we will inevitably make decisions about the path we will take and its direction.

This is not an act of guilt; it is an act of wisdom that seeks true human joy and peace. Just as our guide would have decided to go elsewhere had he surveyed the campground by day, we will decide to turn aside when the light of God's grace upon our path illuminates old familiar ground, and tells us that there are dangerous loose spots in our way. It doesn't matter that we walked over the ground before and either didn't notice the slipping earth or now see that things have changed since we last traversed the ground. We find that the new information from the light causes a new choice.

How can people say they live in God's light, asks John, and then not make choices, and continually correct their actions by continually demonstrating a growing appreciation for other people?

John concludes that these agnostics have not realized the cause of the light. They have not taken it into their lives so they can have it light their path, grasp the reality of it, and make it work for themselves and others.

So what happens if we do say having the light on is a good idea? We must then take the time, put in the effort to embrace the Gospel and lift from it the light of Jesus Christ. The message is that we are all sons and daughters of God, destined to be truly human and have peace and fulfillment when we live with his loving spirit as our guide.

John says when the lights come on; first we begin to have fellowship with one another. Frankly, that's not so hard to understand.

I knew a man and woman once who conceived a child that was in great difficulty early in the pregnancy. The mother of the child began to build up life threatening toxins and it was clear that, unless this baby were taken from her womb three months in advance of her due date, both she and the baby would die. This was a longed for and loved child. The mother waited until the very last possible second before she agreed to the C-section to remove the child.

The child was obviously far from term and was placed on every machine known to medicine that would sustain its life. I clearly remember seeing the baby who was so tiny I could scarcely believe it was real. It looked like a part of the machine that sustained its tiny flickering spirit. The father's obvious love and connection to this precarious life left me speechless with emotion. He then said something to me I have never forgotten.

He said that having this little son under these conditions made him suddenly realize how great God's gift of life was. It made him also aware of how wonderful it was in every human being.

He said that he found himself looking at everyone differently, people in the hospital, and people on the street. Even when he was driving, he found himself cautious in a new way. Not just for himself but for all the gifts of God speeding around him in the dark. "Funny," he said, "having this experience makes me more at ease with people--and, no offense, but even with you, pastor."

An experience with the light of God had touched my friend. It caused him to change course. The question for him, for all of us, is how we keep up the course correction as we travel in life. John answers that we must continually keep the cause of light with us so we can illuminate each situation and try to see it as Christ would have seen it.

Faith in God, faith in the way of Jesus Christ is a dynamic, ever-growing quantity and quality of life. John reflects the fact that living in the light is not fun and games. We become ever aware of our shortcomings; just as a scholar becomes aware of what he doesn't know the more knowledgeable he becomes. The result could be utter frustration. So John adds the clause --"and the blood of Jesus Christ cleanses us from all sin."

That is to say, the Christ we so venerate in the Christmas season is not just the light upon our path, but the promise of acceptance even when we don't see the pitfalls or stumble over them by misjudging our strength. The source of light illuminates the landscape and encourages us to become strong by walking in it, even though we are bound to make mistakes. Jesus tells us that all we have to do is admit the mistakes, seek to understand what they mean for our future, and move on resolved not to make them again.

The experience of the light changes us--but the change, though agonizing at times, is like the agony of birth.

With the lights on, our lives begin to work, our souls begin to function. We can make choices and set priorities, give up some things and grasp others without a desperate feeling that we are missing out.
In his poem, "Journey of the Magi," T.S. Eliot speculates on what it must have felt like for the wise men to see the Light of God in the common stable, and then see their own lives and families sights after that experience. He writes that he thought the experience had altered them and given them a hunger they had only an idea of before they saw the incarnate Spirit of God. He writes these thoughts of one Magi:

> We returned to our places, these Kingdoms,
> But no longer at ease here, in the old dispensation,

When we allow our faith in God that is brought to life in his incarnation in Jesus to illuminate our experiences, we make a choice about living. We choose not to live in the dark that is suitable for sleeping; in Christ we choose to live in the light, and in so doing choose to be awake in our souls.

Christmas invites us to live awakened in the Light of God's Grace in Jesus Christ. May our joy be completed in the year to come by exploring the world that is shown to us by the daylight of Christ's Spirit.

God's Mothering

May 9, 1993

Luke 2:41-52,

John 19:21-27

When Jesus died upon the cross, he died for all humankind. But in the midst of his execution, there was one person whom Jesus was particularly concerned about. Barely able to speak, He reached out from his dying agony to provide for the welfare of his mother, Mary.

From the New Testament, we know that Mary had borne him into the world and endured the questions about the strange circumstances of his birth. When he was a young boy, she had tried to reprimand him in the temple when he was arguing with the learned men of the synagogue. She was there when he made sure everyone at a wedding had enough drink to complete the festivities. She had sent his brothers to try to reason with him when he was becoming infamous for his speeches which were anything but orthodox. He hadn't come home to her, and she had to console herself alone because apparently by that time her husband Joseph had died.

Mary had witnessed her own children gradually won over by their elder brother, James becoming a leader in the Jerusalem church. And she saw her son arrested, tried, and executed before her eyes. Most likely she saw him risen, and experienced the coming of the Holy Spirit on the day of Pentecost when she and her children were praying with the disciples.

We know nothing more about Mary, save what legends, not included in the New Testament, tell us. While these are not considered true in any historical sense, these legends are clearly reflections of both the interest the church had in Mary and the interest Christians have always had in the mothering aspect of God reflected in these legends.

One of these legends was called the *Protevangelion* and was attributed to the hand of James, the brother of Jesus, the first Bishop of Jerusalem. This work says that Mary's parents were Joachim and Anna, a rich aging couple who had no children and were sorely distressed by this. Having been prevented from offering a sacrifice because of his childlessness, Joachim retired to the desert to fast and pray and seek an answer to the cause of his childlessness.

At the same time Anna was beseeching God about her childlessness following a disturbing conversation with her maid. Anna put on her wedding dress and sat under a laurel tree to pray. While she prayed an angel of the Lord appeared to her telling her that her prayers had been answered and that she would bear a child. The angel bid her go to meet her husband who had also been visited by an angel with this news.

Anna promised that her child would be dedicated to the work of the temple as a virgin, just like Samuel. And when Mary was born and named, there was tremendous rejoicing and happiness.

The legend goes on to describe how Mary at nine months old was placed on the ground to see if she could stand. Miraculously, she could not only stand but took nine steps and came to her mother.

Mary was presented in the temple as a one-year-old with great thanksgiving, her father praying thus:

"God of our fathers, bless this girl, and give her a name famous and lasting through all generations. And all the people replied, 'So be it, Amen. "

The legend continues saying that when Mary was three, her parents fulfilled their vow to have her raised in the temple. While she lived in the temple, the legend says, she was fed by angels and spoke often to the messengers of God. When she was 12 years old, Zachariah the priest while in prayer, was told by an angel to gather all of the widowers of Judea so that one of them might be chosen as the husband of Mary.

All of the widowers of Judea were summoned to the temple and were instructed to bring with them their walking staffs. Joseph, hearing the crier summons, threw down the hatchet he had been using, took up his staff and started for the temple. When he stood in the assembly, the priest collected all of the rods, prayed over them, then one by one gave them back to the owners. Nothing happened until the last rod was given back: the rod of Joseph. A dove sprang from the top of the rod and landed on Joseph's head, a sign of the choice of God for the husband of Mary.

Joseph was incredulous, protesting that he was already old and had children to care for and she was a young woman, just 14 years old. The priest insisted, reminding Joseph of God's wrath. Joseph finally consented and obeyed the desire of the priest and became Mary's betrothed.

Reluctantly taking Mary to his home, Joseph explained that he had to be away for some time (over 6 months in fact) tending to his trade. During his absence Mary was visited by the Angel of the Lord and made aware of her call to bear the child of God. So when Joseph returned from his building trip, he found Mary 6 months pregnant. Obviously he was upset, but was convinced of her miraculous pregnancy by the Angel of the Lord.

The legend embellishes the traditional story further when it adds that Joseph and Mary were hauled before the authorities for inquiry about conduct. They explained their circumstances to the unbelieving temple authority. Joseph was given the holy water to drink, water which was supposed to make him sick or kill him if he was lying. But he lived and the couple was vindicated.

After Jesus' birth legend continues to fill in details not included in our Gospels. One legend called the 'First Gospel of the Infancy of Jesus' tells of Mary's miraculous use of her son's power. In one of these stories a woman, also named Mary, was married to a man who also had a second wife who was very jealous of her.

Mary's young son, Galeb fell ill from a fever, and his mother took him to Mary, the Mother of Jesus, upon hearing of miracles the woman had performed for others. Jesus' mother took pity on the hapless Mary, and made a coat from the swaddling cloths of Jesus and placed it on Caleb. Instantly her son was cured. But this did nothing for the jealousy of the other wife. When tending a hot oven Mary was called away, leaving Caleb near her work. The other wife quietly stole into the room in Mary's absence and threw little Caleb into the hot oven, and quickly left the room.

However, when Mary returned she found Caleb happily playing in the oven which was as cold as though it had not been used in weeks, the jealous wife tried again. This time she found Caleb alone, and tossed him down a well. But again the child was saved, and Mary found him happily sitting on top of the water.

The jealous wife was not so lucky. When she tried to examine the well to determine her mistake, she caught her foot on the well rope, fell into the well and drowned.

This same legend gives Mary power of her own, describing a time when Joseph and Mary were traveling in Egypt and entered a city where there was a woman possessed with an evil spirit. She had been stricken with madness which caused her to roam about the desert places naked, breaking restraining chains or cords with which her family tried to bind her. In this state she would appear at the cross roads and churchyards and throw stones at men passing by.

When Mary saw the woman she pitied her, and the very power of her gaze drove the spirit from the woman. The spirit was seen leaving her in the form of a young man who was crying, "Woe to me, because of thee, Mary, and thy son."

These stories, mostly Gnostic stories, were obviously just some of the legends which became the impetus for the Roman Catholic Church's veneration of Mary. This veneration was a way to make tangible something Christians found in Christ, which they attributed to his mother. Although we Protestants gave up the veneration of Mary we have not given up the notion that the character of God is highly charged with "mothering", and that this nurturing spirit exists in humans as one of God's greatest gifts to our souls.

There is a Mary Spirit in all of us. I think she is generally more accessible by women, and she is too often denied by men. She is the spirit that demonstrates to the world what Jesus taught us about the love of God, the Good Shepherd, and the prodigal's parent.

She is the spirit in us that yearns to keep track of birthdays and anniversaries; to make sure that people are given warm hospitality and made to feel welcome and accepted. She is the relationship between work and family.

She is the spirit which seeks to house her family. She is the spirit which values homemaking as much as bridge building or stock trading. She is a mentoring spirit; she views young people with anticipation of their potential. She values time with friends and never thinks of it as a waste even when nothing grand is done or thought or learned.

She delights in watching over those she loves, doing for them, being with them. She nurtures with food, telephone calls, visits, cards and letters, unexpected little gifts, and quiet sacrifices.

God is Mother as well as Father. May we be glad of the mothering God puts into all of our souls. We need to acknowledge it, love it, and let it bear fruit for the world.

Joining the Priesthood

December 4, 1988

I Peter 2: 4-17

Have you seen those bumper stickers on the backs of trucks and vans which ask," How Am I Driving?" They invite you to report good or bad driving to the employing company. I wonder if anyone has ever responded to such an invitation.

I wonder what would happen if we put signs on our cars, office desks, or workstation that said, "Hi, I'm a Christian of the Presbyterian species. How am I'm treating you? Report to 447-2083."

Interestingly, people do take me aside as your pastor and tell me all sorts of things about your conduct. Mostly, I hear things like, "if ever there was a Christian, it is Tom or Eleanor. They are so patient and kind and I can trust them with my life." Other times, I hear, "Joe goes to your church, doesn't he? Well, you ought to do something about him because he may be a good sort when he warms a pew on Sunday but he is one first class jerk at work."

Being Christians is never a private matter. We learned this from the very beginning of the faith.

The letter known as I Peter gives us some of the most meaningful clues about how to think of our community life. Biblical scholars believe this letter was written by the apostle Peter and addressed to the churches in the provinces of Pontus, Galatia, Cappadocia, Asia, and Bithynia. The intent of this letter was to be a circular letter, which went to many churches, and not just one church. Furthermore, evidence suggests that Peter wrote the letter in Rome just before the terrible persecutions of Christians under emperor Nero. With hostility toward Christians in official quarters rising, Peter wrote to the churches of Anatolia to brace for trouble. And sure enough, when it came it was terrible, and probably claimed Peter's life.

In the first chapter of the letter, Peter greets the churches and warns them that they may have to face suffering for their faith. He tells the churches to set their hopes fully upon the revelation of Jesus Christ yet to come and not be conformed to what he calls the "passions of your former ignorance".

Peter exhorts his flocks in verse 15, "but as he who called you is holy, be holy yourselves in all your conduct since it is written, "you shall be holy, for I am holy." Peter tells the churches that when persecution looms, and non-believers are watching what is happening to Christians, they must be careful to model the holiness and love which Christ had called them to experience and share.

Peter points out that though Jesus was rejected as a stone that a builder throws out and the workmen stumble over it, Christ has become the cornerstone in the building of the kingdom of God. Verse 4 says, "Come to him, to that living stone, rejected by men but in God's sight chosen and precious."

Peter exhorts Christians to see themselves as living stones, which God has used to build a spiritual house. Since a temple is consecrated, so Christians are each consecrated as parts of God's action for the good of all people. To be consecrated as a human being is to become a priest. This is the origin of our concept of the priesthood of all believers. Priests were ordained to offer sacrifices to God and seek intercession for the people. Peter broadens this concept of intercession and says that Christians are to see themselves as priests whose offering to God is their work to make the reconciling love and faith in Jesus Christ available to others.

This is what characterizes the church of Jesus Christ. It is not a building or a denomination. It is the totality of human beings who believe in the Lord. They are the new Israel, which is consecrated to act as the priests of the faith drawing others to the grace and peace of Jesus Christ.

What these priests do in the world is extremely important since their actions are their offerings to God. Peter writes that it is extremely important for the churches of Anatolia to be a witness to the love and justice and peace of God when persecution looms. We are facing persecution like the churches of Anatolia, but we are still called to be the priesthood of believers who offer our lives to the work of God's Kingdom. What we do in our community speaks for what we believe about the grace and mercy and the love of God.

Being a Christian can never be just a private matter when we understand that all followers of Christ are consecrated as priests. A priest has to think about, pray about, and act on behalf of the need of others to experience the love and grace of Jesus Christ.

When those of you who are teachers believe that your children are precious souls in who exists a part of God, and students feel their worth in your love and respect, you act as priest. You offer to God your hard work to make his love tangible by being patient, by counseling parents, by risking being so public in your teaching and discipline.

When you volunteer in the school or other community projects, you act from the position of your priesthood. When you remove yourself from petty squabbling and backbiting and competition, which can easily enter even these projects of such benevolent intent, you act as God's priest. The Latin word for "priest" is *pontifex* and it means bridge builder. A priest is to be a builder of bridges between human beings and the love and grace of God. By seeking to work openhandedly and graciously you build bridges to God. When we forget and work angrily, and revengefully, we can easily destroy those bridges.

When those of you who work in business, deal open-handedly and fairly with clients, you demonstrate to God your gift of his priesthood. Treating people in fairness and justice is letting them feel the touch of God.

The opposite is true also. When we treat people unfairly or arrogantly or unjustly and it is clear that we claim to be in the priesthood of believers, we raise credibility questions about our faith.

Let us remember not to confuse being holy with piety. Jesus warned of practicing piety before others just to be seen by them. He taught that there would be no reward for such actions. Holy refers to the difference which exists when we act from the desire that emanates from the part of us that is connected to God's loving grace, mercy and justice and not from our ego and need to be admired. Because each one of us is different, we will express that loving grace in many ways.

Let your light so shine before all, so they may see your good work and give praise to your Father in heaven.

First Fruits of the Tree of Life

March 12, 1995

Genesis 2:10-15; 3:22-24

I am a person who loves the metaphor and imagery of the Bible. When I think of what Jesus means to me, and who he was, I think of the picture puzzle which is presented in the second chapter of the book of Genesis. This picture tells me not only who Jesus is; but what we humans are to become.

The story of Genesis was never to be taken as a literal story. It is to be taken as a story which presents us with deep spiritual truths. Discovery of these truths happen when we decode the symbols in the story.

God set a tree in the midst of the Garden of Eden which was the tree of the knowledge of good and evil. We understand this to be the tree of knowledge of the opposites that are present in life. Knowledge in the Old Testament sense is not just acquiring information, it is experiential knowledge; whoever eats of this tree becomes the partaker of the baffling, yet beautiful world of the secular. In short, whoever eats of the tree becomes mortal. The experience of being mortal gives one the knowledge of both life and death, power and powerlessness. It is the fruit which ends innocence and begins wisdom.

Having eaten of this tree, Genesis tells us, one lacks only one element in being Godlike. The key to this comes from God when he says, "Behold, the man has become like one of us, knowing good and evil. And now, lest he put forth his hand and take also of the tree of life, and eat and live forever. . ."

So God put a flaming sword and Cherubim before the tree of life to guard it from the man and woman lest they approach before they are ready. But what will make them ready? The answer is in the Cherubim, the heavenly creature chosen to guard the tree.

Cherubim are grand creatures who guard holy places. They have wings and four faces: the face of a man; the face of an eagle; the face of an ox; and the face of a lion. To pass the guarding cherubim, one must contain the four aspects of the spirits represented by the four faces.

These signs are: Humanity, symbolized by the human face; Deity, an aspect of the divine, symbolized by the eagle; Humility and sacrificial giving, represented by the ox; and finally a sense of confidence in the strength and power of God, symbolized by the lion.

These are the four aspects of wholeness which we see in the being of Jesus Christ who is the wholeness of God dwelling in a human life. The four aspects of Christ's wholeness are: Christ, the man; Christ who is God; Christ the Lamb of God, who gave His life for the sins of the World; and Christ the King.

These are the four aspects of wholeness, which we need to see in our lives if we want to truly manifest the Christ in us.

THE HUMAN BEING

First we must have in us the humanness of Christ. This means that we must affirm our humanness with all of its joy and suffering as the gift of God. We must learn its limitations as well as its strengths. We need to experience and affirm the human need for love, justice, forgiveness, dignity, and most of all, grace. More importantly, we need to experience the human dependence on the will of God.

In his book, *Exile and Homecoming*, Sam Keene describes the irony of his pursuit of his major goal in life, to earn a Ph. D. and become a professor. In good American fashion, he proceeded to postpone all present satisfactions in the name of reaching that goal. He speaks of failing to cultivate the soil of his own experience, of becoming "an intellectual sharecropper on the fields of absentee landlords." It is one form of experience so familiar to us all. We tend to project our joys and hopes into the future by saying, "As soon as I get the mortgage paid, I will do this and that and satisfaction will be mine."

Keene eventually got his degree and began to be called Doctor and hired as a professor, but he found that the magic he had hoped for did not flood in. Ironically, waves of disillusionment washed over him. In desperation, he cried out, "What can I do that will give dignity and meaning to my life?"

One night in a Manhattan hotel room, Keene awoke with the answer impressed on his mind. The answer to his burning question was, "Nothing, nothing at all."

What Keene realized was that he needed to accept the gracious love of God all around him as a gift, for which he could do nothing. Whatever he did choose to do, he did out of the joy and gratitude of receiving the gift. Keene had begun to truly experience his humanness which gave Jesus the title "Son of Man."

DEITY - DIVINITY

There is a second aspect of Christ in us, which we must seek to manifest if we are to be whole. It is represented by the second face of the Cherubim. We must manifest the sense of Deity or Divinity. This is the Divine Christ in us. This manifestation happens when we see the world and all in it with the same great joy and love that God sees it. When we do, we see in life the great value for which God sent Jesus to redeem the world.

There is a famous poem called "The Touch of the Master's Hand" which gives an idea of what it is like to manifest this sense of the divine. The poem tells of a violin being auctioned off and the most the auctioneer could get for it was three dollars. The auctioneer was declaring that it was going once, going twice, and about to go for three dollars, when a gray-haired man from the back of the room stepped forward, dusted off the instrument, tuned it, and began to play. When he was finished playing, so the poem says, the violin sold for $3,000 instead of $3.00

The poem concludes:

> *What changed its worth?" the man replied:*
> *The touch of the master's hand.*

To see things touched by the master's hand is to manifest the deity of Christ in us, which makes us fit for the tree of life.

THE LION

To be fit for the tree of life we must manifest in our souls the power of God, the notion that we are regal in his eyes. This is the aspect of wholeness represented by the lion, often described as the king of beasts. Christ manifested his sense of majesty in God's eyes in his confidence in dealing with people. This power showed up in the apostles after Jesus' resurrection when they stopped thinking of themselves as powerless followers and claimed their citizenship in the Kingdom of God and began to change the world.

A pastor in the State of Washington tells of a fellow seminary student of his when attending Iliff School of Theology in Denver. The student was failing academically; after six years in school he was still at the bottom of the class. He did have a license to preach, however, and served several small churches around Denver while going to school. But his lack of academic skill made him a washout in these churches. So finally in desperation his Bishop sent him to the parish no one wanted, a little parish way up in the Rocky Mountains in a coal-mining field.

This man believed in the power of God, and that it could flow even through his non-academically oriented brain. In that little coalmining town in which no trained student wanted to stay and preach, the power of God began to flow in his life. He was the only pastor the town ever had who would crawl down into the mine shaft during a cave-in and read scripture to the trapped miners. He was the only pastor they ever had who would be out on the picket line on cold mornings serving coffee and trying to bring peace and reconciliation to troubled labor relations.

He had lots of problems: his wife fell ill; his car began to fall apart, the parsonage roof burned and while he was trying to fix it he slipped and broke his leg.

When he finally had to leave, the mine closed for the day, ceasing its operation so that the people could cram into the church to show him their love. People had to stand outside open windows to hear what was going on because of the crush of the people who wanted to show this man how much he was appreciated.

When the last hymn was sung, a big Polish miner came up to the pulpit with a hat filled with money, he put his arms around the pastor and said: "Preach... Us guys love you. We give you this." He handed the pastor the money and gave him a great Polish, bone popping hug.

The pastor felt it in more ways than one. He felt the transforming power of God alive in him and his parish. He went on to work as a Lay Pastor serving churches in North Dakota. The man knew in his heart that even though he never would shine on a test in an academic setting, God marked him as worthy as any king on earth to bear his grace and power to the world around him.

THE OX

If we are to be fit to eat of the tree of life, we must fix in our lives the experience of sacrificial living and giving. Jesus said "He who gains his life will lose it, and he who loses his life for my sake will gain it." When we give things away out of love and faith, we are not losing anything, we are gaining far more than what we gave away.

In a book called *Friendly Anecdotes,* there is a story told of a Quaker sea captain named Gifford who transported coal from Philadelphia to the Atlantic seaport town of Nantucket. One severe winter there was a coal shortage and when his coal-laden ship arrived, he had no sooner dropped anchor than a coal merchant came aboard and offered to buy the whole cargo at $12 a ton. Captain Gifford did not hesitate to turn the tempting offer down. He knew it would be unfair, and would cost people dearly since the merchant was out to make a handsome profit because of the shortage. Even though it entailed extra days in port and extra record keeping, the Quaker captain sold his shipment as always at one ton per customer and at the prevailing price of $8 a ton. He called it "acting conscience." It was acting holiness, as well.

Why not taste of the four aspects of Christ in your life? Then you can be robust with the health that comes from eating of the tree of life. It is a meal of the spirit, which lasts for all eternity.

Discerning the Prophetic

January 29, 2006

When I was entering high school at age 13, I was on a pretty tight budget because there was not a lot of extra money in my single-parent home. When I decided I wanted to listen to music beyond the selections available on my "superhetrodyne radio receiver," I went down to the local record shop to find either a 33-1/3 speed album or a single 45 rpm record of songs I wanted to enjoy.

In that year Elvis Presley was high on the charts belting out "All Shook Up" and "Jail House Rock". But I wasn't much of a Presley fan and I wasn't into Frank Sinatra crooning "Witchcraft". It sounded like someone my mom would like to listen to and I couldn't have that. Pat Boone was singing "Love Letters in the Sand" and "April Love" but I was just a 9th grade geek and not yet into exploring my feelings for girls. Little Richard was doing an energetic performance in "Tutti Fruitti", Buddy Holley had just come out with "Peggy Sue" and I was a bit more interested in their manly renditions. What truly caught my attention was a talented performer: Fats Domino singing "Blueberry Hill".

This was my kind of popular music singer and song. It was a straight-forward; understandable beat that sounded like our semi-automatic washing machine on hard wash cycle. For some reason the 45 rpm record was more expensive than the song listed on a LP I found in the bargain rack, where "Blueberry Hill" was buried in a jumble of songs by country western swing singers. This seemed a bit strange to me, but I counted it as an accidental bonanza. So I bought the cheap album.

My plan was to put the album on my record player and skip right to Fats belting out "I found my thrill on Blueberry Hill ..." I sat down after finding the right track on the LP and starting the needle on its way, waiting to hear Fats Domino's incredibly rich voice punching out the words to that great song.

What a shock. Instead of hearing rhythm and blues with sax, piano, drums and bass, the song started with guitars and an unmistakable tone of western he-haw twang! It was Gene Autry singing Blueberry Hill in a western swing style and in my estimation, positive ruining it.

I was completely flabbergasted. I was not aware that Blueberry Hill had originally been heard in Autry's 1940s movie "Singing Hills." Or that Glenn Miller had done a rendition of it, followed by Louis Armstrong and finally my hero, Fats Domino. All I knew was that this was not the authentic Blueberry Hill I needed to hear!

This experience of my past came to mind as I thought about scripture passages that deal with the issue of identifying false and real prophets. What is a true prophet? How is he or she different from a false prophet?

Paul teaches us in the second chapter of First Corinthians that, "The unspiritual man does not receive the gifts of the Spirit of God, for they are folly to him, and he is not able to understand them because they are spiritually discerned." Paul goes on to list the gifts of the spirit, which includes the gift of prophesy.

What we have discovered about spiritual life since the time Moses led the Exodus and Jesus cast out demons in the synagogue is that the prophetic Spirit of God can fall on all of us at times. What is necessary is for us to allow it to come forth and to also recognize it in others. If we look at the stories of Moses and Jesus we can discover certain characteristics in the believers around them. They were people who were open to the transmittal of the spirit they saw in Moses and in Jesus and they knew without a doubt that the Spirit of God was really at work.

For all of his charming and melodious twang, I could quickly discern that Gene Autry wasn't Fats Domino. Likewise, let us put on the mind of Christ and listen with our hearts and spiritual consciousness in prayer and meditation. We will be able to quickly discern who speaks for God and who is just masquerading; the true voice of the prophet will resonate within us. The wonderful outcome of this fervent listening for the true spirit is the ability to stop masquerading ourselves.

A Bend in the Road

March 7, 1993

You have probably seen this family scenario many times; perhaps in your own family. There are two sons who grow up together in a family with a parent who is very hard to please. One son decides that the way to gain attention from his parent is to rebel. He chooses to do everything that is opposite to what his parent wants him to do. His anger is transparent, hurtful and destructive to himself and others.

The other boy does all he can to conform to his parents' hard demands. He is the good boy who strives to be the best in the eyes of the family. In his striving to be perfect he pushes issues to the limit and then beyond. He believes he is good and will not accept anyone who is not. He is also full of anger but it becomes masked as righteous indignation. He has hidden anger at the tyranny of having to please in an environment where he can never be sure that he has pleased enough. He externalizes the anger at those who are beneath his idea of goodness.

The writer of the famous hymn, "Amazing Grace," was John Newton. John Newton and the apostle Paul were those kinds of people - Newton the rebel, Paul the pleaser.

In Jewish theology in Saul's day, many believed that a human had to earn the favor of God by following the law. This tradition held that the great patriarch Abraham, though he did not know of the written law, knew by intuition the law and its tenants. By following this intuitive law he gained favor with God and became the ancestor of all Judaism. They believed that this was an example that the way to gain the attention of God was to obey the many laws of God.

There was in Saul's time a small party of Pharisees who believed differently. This party wrote in a rabbinic commentary of Abraham, "Abraham, our father, inherited this world and the world to come solely by the merit of faith whereby he believed in the Lord; for it is said, "And he believed in the Lord, and he accounted it to him for righteousness."

But this was a minority view. Saul (Paul) belonged with the majority party with a vengeance that appeared as if Saul was trying to please an unnamed inner voice, probably a parent. He was the consummate zealot who was filled with righteous indignation at anyone who would deny the tenants of the law much less fail to follow them. He believed such an act was so abominable that it was deserving of the ultimate punishment.

Saul (Paul) was the religious fundamentalist Shiite of his day. There is little difference between the zealous, self-righteous Saul and the perpetrators of the destruction of the world trade center. Mohammed

Salameh and his associates belonged to a sect of Muslims who believed so fervently in their religious doctrine, they taught that foreigners who come to their country and seek out the cheap purchase of carnal pleasures, alcohol, drugs and all of its evils, deserved death for corrupting their religious life. They believed that American tourists were bringing a barrage of secularism to Egypt. The message of destruction they sent to America was to declare that its decadence would not be without terrible cost.

Saul believed that corruption of traditional Jewish religious practice was the corruption of the will of God. Behind this deadly zealousness in Saul was a dark shadow filled with inner rage and disappointment which couldn't be appeased - an anger seeking an avenue of expression in religious fanaticism.

After Saul had seen to it that Steven, a Christian, was stoned to death, he set out to destroy as many Christians as he could legally lay hands upon. As he rode to Damascus to launch his deadly program of pious persecution, he was suddenly blinded by the presence of the risen Christ, and Christ's gentle but compelling words, "Saul, Why do you persecute me?"

Saul fell into blindness and depression. He could never have imagined that God would declare his enemies right about who Jesus was, and that his passion for religious law was so terribly wrong and abhorrent to God. In his trying to be so right, he had actually been horribly wrong.

While he was in Damascus, he was cared for by a Christian named Ananias, who ministered so lovingly to the man whose fearful reputation had preceded him. Instead of anger Saul received grace, mercy, forgiveness, and the invitation to start his life again.

Paul's entire view of life and himself changed! He realized that he could not always please those around him. He could not measure up to people's expectations all of the time. Knowing that God accepted him, he chose to live by grace. Later, when he wrote to the church at Rome he was trying to convey the same truth about Abraham.

Abraham wasn't the most perfect man in the world. He grew in his goodness because he had accepted God's grace. He was certainly a man of weaknesses at times. He had allowed his own son to be driven away from him by Sarah's jealousy. He had risked Sarah's life by having her pretend to be his sister when he sojourned in Egypt; he feared the worst if she traveled as his beautiful wife.

But he was a man who knew the grace of God and allowed that grace to penetrate his life and his point of view. Because of receiving God's graciousness in his being, he could accept God's promises as possible.

The grace of God is received by Christians as the gift of God. Its aim is the healing of the very deepest and darkest parts of our soul and where the shadowy impulses in our lives operate against our best laid plans. Grace does not require us to do anything to earn God's love. Once it is accepted deep within, it begins to work on us so that out of our joy and gladness we find the healing power of his grace.

John Newton, the writer of the hymn, "Amazing Grace" represents another experience of the power of grace in a human's life. It was so powerful that in his quiet way, Newton helped end slavery in England.

Newton was the son who rebelled against his parent. Newton was the son of a sea captain, doubtless a man who knew how to make known what he expected. After Newton's mother died when he was seven and his father remarried, he was sent to boarding school. He left at the age of ten because of the strict discipline which nearly broke his spirit.

He went to sea with his father at age eleven and was known as a lad who was rebellious yet had times of religious calm and nostalgia for his home. Deep down he was still hurt and angry about the world that had taken his mother, abandoned him to boarding school, and given him a father with expectations he didn't think he could fulfill.

In 1743, he was pressed into service aboard a "Man o' War." Even though his father used his influence to make him a midshipman, Newton so hated the life that he again rebelled and was whipped publicly, chained and demoted to a common seaman.

This disgrace made him bitter and the Man o' War was glad to get rid of him when they arrange his transfer to a slave ship bound for Africa. Once there, he quit the ship and took service with a white slave dealer on an island off Sierra Leone. This proved to be a hard and merciless life in which he knew deprivation and great cruelty, as well as reckless abandon.

At the request of his father, another sea captain took Newton off the island and on a voyage that went to Brazil and back to England via the Newfoundland Banks. On the trip Newton read Thomas Kempis' *Imitation of Christ* and the book made him think anew about the state of his life and God in his life. During a terrible storm in which he feared the boat would sink and he would surely drown because he could not swim, he fell into a terrible fear about the state of his soul and his relationship to God. At that time he received the grace of God offered in Christ, and counted himself a believer in the saving power of God.

Newton then got his act together and became captain of his own slave ship. Believing that what God had done in his own life God could do in the lives of his crew, Newton held public worship aboard ship. But the person most changed by this worship was probably not the crew, but Newton himself.

Later in the book of Romans, Paul declares it is faith that gives us fellowship with God, not righteous action. Paul says that the works of grace are the outcome of the healing of the soul not the cause of the healing. Newton certainly proved this.

As Newton lived his Christian life in the then socially sanctioned task of captaining a slave ship, he began to see his human cargo differently. Before long he was troubled by his involvement even when he saw to it that they were humanely treated aboard his ship. Humane treatment notwithstanding, he still delivered innocent people to bondage and servitude as though they were criminals. Whereas once he saw slaves as subhuman and an avenue for the venting of his inner wrath at life's cruelty, now he could only see them as suffering human beings, people bound in misery as he had once been.

Newton left the slave trade around 1754 and lived as a tide surveyor at the port of Liverpool while studying diligently for the ministry. His rough background and inability to feign an air of English snobbery in his role as cleric kept his well established Bishop from ordaining him until 1764. He was then ordained by the Bishop of Lincoln and sent to minister in the little village of Olney where he remained for the next 15 years.

His past experiences made him sympathetic to the plight of his congregation and he so earnestly ministered to common folk that his services were jammed with people. He became an open opponent of slave trading, preaching about its misery and its power to stoke the darkness in human beings and to obscure the blessings of God.

After he was transferred from Olney to a London Church where he ministered until his death in 1807, he became acquainted with the famous parliamentarian, Wil Wilburforce. Their friendship was one of the key elements that converted Wilburforce from a passive faith in God to an active faith based upon the grace of God. And it was clearly Newton who persuaded Wilburforce that Christians who were saved by the grace of God could not in good conscience enslave other human beings.

In the last year of Newton's life, his religious protégé, Wil Wilburforce, succeeded in putting through

Parliament a bill that abolished slavery in England forever.

Grace is a powerful healing agent. If we take it even in small doses often enough, it takes the pain away from the deepest of our losses, the anxiety out of the worst of our fears, and the hurt from the most terrible of disappointments.

Grace does not prescribe specific action as though it is God's law. But it does bring inner peace and the knowledge of what God has done and can do through us. Through his grace, we can be free of inner turmoil, anger and fear.

Newton, who was more remarkable for his goodness than his greatness, said at age 82:, "My memory is nearly gone, but I remember two things, that I am a great sinner, and that Christ is a great Savior."

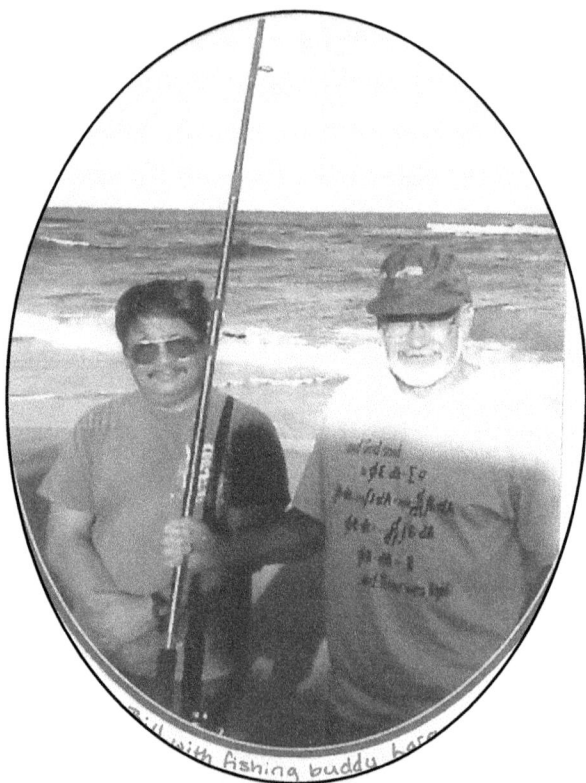

I enjoy fishing—especially with my buddy Larry

God is Not Complacent

December 8. 1985

Colossians 1:15-20

Do you remember the book and film, which were titled, *"The Right Stuff"*? If you'll remember they dealt with the selecting and training of America's astronauts. The term., "The Right Stuff" referred to the characteristics, attitudes, and spirit if you will, which were necessary for a person to possess in order to be an astronaut.

In the end, it all seemed pretty machismo to me, because so much of the right stuff had to do with physical strength, technical knowhow, and the ability for one to stay cool while being stalked by death. In one part of the book, an astronaut becomes frightened when things begin to go wrong in a mission where he made some serious mistakes. His welcome back to earth was greatly cooled off by his loss of nerve. Obviously, as the book implied, he was not made of the right stuff.

Interestingly, as seen through the eyes of the Good News, it was the wrong stuff that made those around this astronaut fail to even give thanks that he had returned to earth alive.

I think what always disturbs me about rave reviews of having the right stuff portrayed in the book is that such judgments start to leak over into other situations in life where they don't belong. They do so because we humans seem to be on a constant quest for what is the right stuff in us, not just the right stuff for being an astronaut (or something as heroic), but for being a human being. In the end, I suppose many think that having the right stuff will result in the fullest life.

Paul says some things to us about the right stuff in the book of Colossians:

> He is the image of the unseen God and the first-born of all creation, for in him were created all things in heaven and on earth: everything visible and everything invisible. Thrones, Dominations, Sovereignties, Powers - all things were created through him and for him. Before anything was created, he existed. And he holds all things in unity. Now the Church is his body, he is its head. As he is the Beginning, he was first to be born from the dead, so that he should be first in every way; because God wanted all perfection to be found in him and all things to be reconciled through him and for him, everything in heaven and everything on earth, when he made peace by his death on the cross.
>
> *Colossians 1:15-20*

Paul's point of view in Colossians is quite clear. Jesus of Nazareth was God incarnate, God taking up residence in a human being. In Paul's mind, Jesus was "the Right Stuff" par excellence. He was the image of the invisible. He was the creative spirit behind every creature: "The first born of every creation."

Every living thing derives from the Spirit of God, which entered the human called Jesus of Nazareth. And so every living thing has in it the Right Stuff.

Paul writes, "And He is before all things and by him all things consist."

Despite the fact that all things are made of what Christ is made of - the Right Stuff - somehow in humanity things have deteriorated to the wrong stuff. Perhaps humanity was using the right stuff in the wrong way - like drinking gas and putting water in one's gas tank. Both elements are the right stuff. But when we have a distorted view of this purpose, they quickly and definitely become the wrong stuff ... and the results let us know about it immediately.

Paul declares that God moved to get creation back to making the right stuff by changing the human viewpoint about the uses, purposes, and powers of the varied stuff of which we are made. We are spiritual beings, formed with a need to have God fill us with the right attitudes, expectations and judgments – indeed to be filled with the right stuff.

Paul continues:
> Because God wanted all perfection to be found in him and all things to be reconciled through him and for him, everything in heaven and everything

on earth, when he made peace by his death on the
cross.

Colossians 1: 20

God came to humans in human form. He spoke to his
people as equals and his words became power. John
discovered that reality and so wrote of Jesus as the
Word of God; the true communication of God, not in
words so much as in action.

God's Word, language in the incarnation, was
consistent with his word and action through the ages.

In the Old Testament, God acted to begin this
declaration of the right stuff and its uses in life. He
spoke, sending a message through action. He took a
scared mommy's boy named "Jacob" and promised to
make of him a special nation, one which would become
a light to all the nations of the world. Jacob hardly
grasped the significance of what God was saying and
acting through him.

God took the orphan waif of the Egyptian court who
couldn't speak without stuttering. Moses had great
doubts that he could stand against the greatest power
on the face of the earth. Yet God acted through him and
made him the greatest leader of the nation of Israel.

He made a covenant with a group of slaves, and desert
riff-raff, who were such nobodies that nobility of the
ancient world would have been horrified to be caught
dead with any of them.

His Spirit entered a woman named Deborah and in a
totally chauvinistic world, he caused her faithfulness to

him to force even the most prejudiced to bless her strength and leadership.

His great prophets were often drawn from the common stuff. There was Elijah, Jeremiah, Amos - all men of no means, all historically invisible if we are looking for those with power, wealth, economic and political clout.

Later, in the fullness of time, God spoke to a teenage girl who was betrothed to an older man in Nazareth. He told her that she would be the mother of His own son, the Messiah. This savior of the world would be God himself in human flesh. Jesus would be the image of the invisible God.

This act, the incarnation, brings God's message to us to its clearest form. God has put "The Right Stuff" in all of us. It is what is common in us, varied in us, and the affirmation of God's spirit in the world.

This business of "The Right Stuff" is an important part of our makeup. I was once a custodian, working my way through seminary. One of my jobs was to open and close a multi-purpose room for a folk dancing class run by the town recreation department.

I remember watching a dignified couple appear one night. Both were dressed well, though casually. Both were in their early 50s, and he seemed most uncomfortable at being there. It was obvious that his greatest fear was that his fun-loving wife would ask him to, of all things, dance. He did not want to appear to be made of the wrong stuff by making a fool of himself by hopping about, clapping his hands, laughing, shaking his body to the rhythm of the music.

His whole demeanor said, "Please don't make me get out there and be found to have the wrong stuff."

Little by little his wife prevailed. Her patience, and obvious love of her thoroughly up -tight husband was remarkable. Her touch, her smile, her non-threatening invitation to him to just walk in the circle with her made him slowly realize that what he was, even though awkward and unskilled, still the right stuff in his wife's eyes. He soon began to enjoy it.

We all have this trouble to some degree; trouble identifying the right stuff in us and using it rightly. Groups of people, even nations have this same worry about the right stuff which influences their actions against others and distorts their lives. Marxists look at the world and declare that everything has to be interpreted in terms of class war. So by definition, the right stuff is anything which is supportive of Marxist thought and the wrong stuff is what is not supportive. So even language gets distorted and oppression is called freedom with obligation.

The invasion of Grenada was an example of our country glorying in martial victory because we had begun as a people to fear that we were no longer made of the right stuff. What was the right stuff we thought we had lost? Was it the power to squash a gnat with a sledgehammer? That is not the right stuff of Christ's Kingdom.

What is the right stuff, we humans wonder. What part of us is worth affirming, praising, and lifting up? The right stuff is our very being, all that we have in us, our love, our intelligence at whatever level, our sense of beauty, our introversion and extraversion, our orderliness and our spontaneity . . . all of these can be the right stuff. Let His spirit channel it and use it, call it forth, or call it back as God directs.

Mary became the willing host of God's Spirit simply by believing that God had affirmed the right stuff for her. Once again, God had declared to humans in the incarnation that it is the commonness in us that God loves and affirms.

We all have plenty of the right stuff in us, which is being used the wrong way, or not being used at all. The result of this is a distancing from God's intention for us; a distancing from what truly satisfies a soul.

You can become a fulfilled human being. You only have to accept that Christ has brought to all humankind the message that our nature is the right stuff when we accept God's love and grace into our lives.

Meeting without Agenda

February 21, 1993

When we examine the meaning of the story of the transfiguration of Jesus Christ on Mt. Hermon, it is helpful to remember that the writer of the gospel of Matthew is intent upon telling us two things: First, that Jesus Christ is the anointed of God, the bearer of God to all generations. Second, Matthew wants us to know the nature of the Messiah, because this will tell of his connection to us, and what he expects us to be.

It is clear that Matthew wants us to understand Jesus as both the promised manifestation of God on earth and to see him as a new Moses, a mediator of the new law, the leader of the new exodus to God's spiritual promise land. The birth narrative of Christ is similar to the birth narrative of Moses. Both babies were sought out to be killed by cruel rulers; both rulers killed first-born sons in an attempt to eliminate threats to their power.

The flight of Joseph and Mary to Egypt and then the return of the family from Egypt to Palestine is seen by Matthew as an echo of the original exodus. In Matthew, Chapter 2 Verse 15 he writes: "This was to fulfill what had been spoken by the Lord through the prophet, 'Out of Egypt I have called my son.'"

Matthew tells us that when Jesus started his Galilean ministry he went to the top of a hill to deliver the beatitudes and the teachings, which included the Lord's Prayer. In this way Matthew lets us know that Christ was the new Moses for the church, the leader of the new exodus from the power of evil and cruelty, the bringer of the new teaching which would lead people to their spiritual salvation.

The story of the transfiguration of Jesus on the 9000 foot heights of Mt. Hermon is full of parallels to the story of Moses meeting God on Mt. Sinai to receive the Law. The book of Exodus reminds us of that story and helps us see these parallels.

When God told Moses to meet him on Mt. Sinai, the glory of the Lord, or the Shechinah settled upon the mountain. God had Moses wait for six days before calling him out of the cloud which enveloped Sinai to proceed to the mountain's crest. The Shechinah is described as a devouring fire. This is the same description we have of the presence of God in the pillar of fire and the shinning cloud, which led the people on the Exodus. It is also the description of the bush, which burned with a seemingly devouring fire but was not consumed. This was the burning bush out of which God's voice called Moses to begin the Exodus.

Also, we should note that Moses spent 40 days on the mountain with God, the same number of days that Jesus spent in the desert, the number of day's characteristic of a great spiritual change in a person's life.

With these parallels in mind let us turn to the drama of the transfiguration. Before Jesus had taken Peter, James and John with him to Mt. Hermon, he had told his disciples that he was going to make the Passover journey to Jerusalem and that he would be killed there, and then he would rise from the dead. Peter couldn't believe what he was hearing and when he resisted such a violent end to his Lord's life, Jesus rebuked him with the famous words "Get behind me Satan".

William Barclay the noted British Biblical scholar says that Jesus goes to the top of Mt. Hermon not just to give his disciples a thrilling look at his Lordship, but rather he goes to the top in order to seek clarity about God's will in what he knows to be a very difficult road ahead of him.

Jesus takes his trusted friends with him and like Moses waits for six days before going to the mountain. I believe these six days are preparation days. Like Moses, Jesus prepares to meet a very important question about himself, God's will, and his decisions.

I would guess that these were reflective days, time to ascertain his own needs and what God wanted of him. This would again be echoed in Gethsemane when Jesus asked God to take the cup of the crucifixion from him if it pleased God, ending the words, "Not my will, but thine be done."

In both narratives these six days are used as a method to obtain spiritual centering. Jesus took this time to gather up his thoughts and to sift them before the light of God's presence, weighing out what his real motivations were and what might be considered his agenda and God's agenda. In this way when he ascended the mountain to meet God he would be clear of some unspoken, maybe hidden inner agenda which would confuse his human will with God's will.

In the book of Revelation John has a vision of Christ and Christ gives him a message to relay to a number of the churches of his day. To the church at Laodicea in what is now Turkey he says to deliver the message that they are lukewarm in their faith. They are tempering the message of God for their lives with their own agendas and this has taken the restorative power out of their faith.

The region around Laodicea was noted for its hot springs which were seen as having healing power. The Romans had built hot baths over these sites and had developed the supposedly restoring and healing ritual of bathing first in the hot baths then plunging into a cold bath.

When John speaks to Laodicea about its lukewarm faith he is saying that the church of Laodicea has become preoccupied with its own agenda so that it cannot do the healing work it is supposed to do in people's lives. God does not jump into their lives like an angry bull, but rather God urges them to open the door of their inner lives and their hearts to him.

> Behold I stand at the door and knock. And if anyone will open the door to me I will come in to him and eat with him, and he will eat with me.
>
> *Revelation 3:20*

God does not enter into the life of a person by force, but rather enters when a person responds to the persistent and loving knock, willingly opens the door and invites

Christ into his inner life. When we do this, we are assured that God will share a spiritual meal with us. The result will be that the fire of life will be stoked in our hearts and we will not only be made whole, but we will have the power to give others spiritual health and wholeness as well.

Ash Wednesday marks the beginning of Lent, a time when we try to do some serious discerning of God's will and seek direction for our lives. When we contemplate the six days that Jesus spent preparing his heart to meet God, we recognize that we also need to spend time preparing our hearts to receive God during lent.

In the book of Revelations Christ tells the Laodocians to let him into their inner being where the motivation and agendas they create for running their lives dwell. He asks that they talk to Him over a meal, a symbol of peace and tranquility, about what they think and feel and want, and then listen to what he might say without feeling threatened or afraid.

The story of the transfiguration gains more personal relevance if we keep this thought in mind as we look at the conclusion of the story. After the six days of preparation to meet God, Jesus takes with him three trusted friends and ascends the hill heights of Mt. Hermon. In Luke we are told that the final meeting of God on the crest happens at night when the disciples are sleeping, and they awake to the glow of the transfiguration. Between these two accounts we are told that the disciples were dumbstruck by the sight of Jesus changed into a being of light, surrounded by a shimmering cloud, the Shechenah, which was represented in the story of Moses as the consuming fire.

Two other figures appear with Jesus. Moses appears, representing the law and Elijah, the prophets. The disciples gazed in wonder at the complete revelation of God: the law, the prophets and the incarnation of God, Jesus Christ.

Peter wanted to enshrine this moment, thinking that the appearance of the Shechanah, the glory of God, meant that the final event of the age had come and they were now in the era of the New Jerusalem. But then the cloud covered them, and Peter stopped as a voice from the cloud gently cautioned him to stop talking about his agenda and listen to what Christ had to say to him.

In the verses just after this event in which Matthew tells us, Jesus is confronted by a distraught father who begs him to heal his epileptic son. He tells Jesus that the disciples apparently hadn't had the power to affect a cure. Jesus then cures the boy and reminds them that with the increase in faith they will have the power to heal.

The word of God urges us to take the spiritual exodus out of darkness. We need to abandoned our private agendas created out of all of our inner hurt and turmoil and confusion over who and what we are. The gospel asks us to take Christ as the shinning Shechanah, or glory of God, the pillar of fire by night and shinning pillar of cloud by day which leads us upon the journey of life God would have us take.

The gospel asks us to let Christ be the law giver of our lives and that the law be not a set of rules written in stone, but a living faith which is nurtured by inviting Christ into the very center of our lives. There we can sup with him and discuss honestly what we are all about, and listen in prayer to his gracious guidance.

So what happens next? After we have met God and let his gracious love restore us and affirm us, God asks us to do as Christ did. We are asked to leave the mountain of contemplation and confront our lives.

Perhaps after putting aside our agenda and taking up God's as the guide of our journey in life, we will meet someone who is in need of healing. To each of us is given the gift of faith, which turns the healing water of our souls boiling hot if we let it do so. Let us meet God during the season of Lent and discern what his agenda is and how it can become our agenda. Let us allow our healing power to meet the needs of our world and rejoice in the glory of God.

Jean and me with young Valerie and Chris

Loose Lips Sink Ships

September 17, 2000

James 3:1-18

I used to think that anytime I recited the now old adage "Loose lips sink ships" most adults knew the meaning and origin of the words. Recently I discovered that one of the members of my own sermon group had somehow missed this saying in her young years. This phrase may not be familiar to you as well. Its origin comes from the Second World War.

During World War II German U-boats operated all over the Atlantic, even just off the coast of our nation. They sank ships within sight of our own land. In fact in those early days of U-boat warfare, the German submariners liked to allow a ship to get near its terminal port, seemingly safe from attack, and then blow it up with a torpedo. Obviously it had a great effect on American morale. This kind of warfare made Allied seafarers wary of letting anyone know their destination or cargo or time of sailing. From a few seemingly innocent comments spoken at a bar or diner, a German spy could piece together the course of a convoy, relay the information to U-boats and cause devastating destruction and possible loss of life. Crews were warned not to speak of their travels to anyone, and the motto "Loose lips sink ships," was soon posted everywhere mariners frequented.

By the time James wrote his letter to the 12 tribes of the Diaspora, meaning the Christian churches, Christianity had attained many decades of experience with the nature of community. Before long it was beset by the greatest of challenges that humans face when they attempt to come together as a Christ-centered group: the challenge of keeping human verbal communication as loving, fair, truthful, and constructive as the intentions of the faith. Before a decade had passed in the faith there were differences in theology that only became more intense and hard to reconcile as time went on. In addition, there were the human proclivities for offensives and defensives which could split a congregation asunder and leave its members trembling with anger and frustration. All said in the name of Christ.

James puts forth his best thinking, none of which is new to us. It is not new news that the tongue or more specifically, the gift of words and language is the most powerful gift humans have to use or squander. Words seem so fragile when they are reduced to weak compressions of air or pen scratches on pieces of paper. But when their content is unleashed by another human brain, the power in those words can launch armies, sink ships, ruin careers, make presidents, or destroy nations.

It's interesting what happens when preachers begin to talk about communicating. I recently logged into the sermon site called "The Desperate Preacher's Site." Mind you this site is specifically planned to accommodate pastors preaching on the subject of James' warning about harsh, unchristian use of the tongue, or more generally, language.

The first entry came from a pastor who shared that he had once seen a children's sermon about the power of the tongue and for an illustration the storyteller brought with him a goat's tongue. Someone else posted the following: "I saw a group of people give a children's sermon. They had something covered and each said it was dangerous, damaging. Then the last person uncovered a real goat's tongue! It was dramatic. I can easily find a cow's tongue, but they are huge, much too big. Does anyone know where I can find a small animal's tongue?" It was signed, "Restless."

Now mind you this is supposed to be a site for preachers desperate to get a handle on an impending sermon; it is not a chat room where we battle out disagreements. The spirit of the forum is to share, ask, and move on. However, the question stirred someone's ire and the writer got this back from another pastor:

"Some children who are vegetarians and their parents might object STRONGLY to the killing of small animals which your 'dramatic' illustration requires." The pastor goes on to suggest that the person use the illustration of fire to demonstrate the destructive quality of the human tongue and ends by saying, "This is an illustration that doesn't require killing things."

Restless replies: "I am sure if Jesus told the parable of the prodigal son you would have been repulsed by the butchering of the fatted calf and missed the point and offended Jesus in the process, just as you so viciously missed the point of this metaphor that James shared. I saw this done 15 years ago and those youth and children grew up knowing how hurtful their words can be. Apparently you never learned that lesson."

As this discussion went back and forth, others joined the fray and then someone wrote, "We need look no further than this week's conversation to see that an unbridled tongue is not reserved to the laity."

James had watched how selfish, insensitive, unthinking and untended communication had messed up church life and made Christians look like hypocrites. What James really wished the church to do was to treat communication as a holy gift. This meant seeing communication as a discipline, which needed to be tended, thought about, prayed over and often reviewed and corrected. It meant not just speaking, but listening and responding or choosing not to respond in measured Christian fashion.

The question James asks of us is whether our communication in our homes, at work, in our neighborhood, in social and political life, and at church, is holy and constructive communication. It can be easy for communication to break down when we don't tend it as a spiritual discipline.

If we don't watch over it we can develop the habit of constantly speaking negatively. We observe the wrong, the bitter, and the dark about everyone and everything. This can happen when we are unhappy with something, and that dark, troubling unhappiness would like to get out and express itself. It leaks out in constant ridicule of certain people, or groups.

Unfortunately, what fuels a person caught in these negative loops are well meaning friends who think it is not their duty to tell this person that their negativity is clearly a sign of their inner distress, not a depiction of someone else's wrongdoing. To be nice we nod our heads, and say things like, "Yeah, I know what you mean." What we really want to say is, "You're really mad about something else entirely and you're just taking it out on yet another unwitting victim."

James speaks of bridling the tongue. He makes the analogy that just as a bridle is a small thing compared to the great animal, a little pressure on the bridle can control the animal's actions. Similarly, the tongue is a small thing compared to the big outcomes it can control if a little pressure is exerted on it by the will. Bridles make horses stop, go, or turn and even back up. So James is saying that we in Christian life need to not just curtail the tongue, but also guide it with loving faith.

James Hewitt relates the following story in his book, *Illustrations Unlimited*: A man and woman were celebrating their golden anniversary - fifty years of married life. Having spent most of the day with relatives and friends at a big party given in their honor, they were home again and decided, before retiring, to have a little snack of tea with bread and butter. They went to the kitchen where the husband opened up a new loaf of bread and handed the end piece (the heel) to his wife. Whereupon she exploded!

She said, "For fifty years you have been dumping the heel of the bread on me. I will not take it anymore. I'm tired of this lack of concern for me." She went on and on in the bitterest of terms about him offering her the heel of the bread. The husband was absolutely astonished at her tirade. When she had finished he said to her quietly, "But it's my favorite piece."

Paul tried to give voice to the nature of Christian love when he wrote to the people of the church in Corinth who were involved in backbiting and speaking ill about one another. His 13th Chapter declares,

> Love is patient and kind, it is not jealous or conceited or proud. Love is not ill-mannered or selfish or irritable; love does not keep a record of wrongs; love is not happy with evil, but is happy with the truth. Love never gives up and its faith, hope and patience never fail.
>
> *1 Corinthians 13:4-7*

If we wanted a Christian mantra to guide our attempts to be a disciple of Jesus in our communication, these words are as perfect a guide as any our faith has produced. Following them requires examination of ourselves, our motives, our ways of doing business, and a willingness to work on filling our communication with the light of God. We need not be sucked into dark communications that foment and spread dissent.

This means attention to not only what we say, but also how we say it. James Dobson once noted a sign posted on a convent in southern California which read: "Absolutely No Trespassing - Violators Will be Prosecuted to the Full Extent of the Law. Signed, "The Sisters of Mercy."

A very important part of being a member of a Christian body and living in our society with thousands of secondary relationships is the way our communication treats all people that enter our lives. We need to know that one of our challenges is to be Christ-like and we should know that when our harsh communication sends a message to the waitress, or clerk, or office help that they are bumbling fools, you don't exactly score points for the cause or bring the touch of Christ to another life.

There is a story of the sailor who was upbraided by the newly commissioned ensign who was at sea for the first time, dying to show off his power and knowledge to someone of inferior rank.

When a seaman carrying a mop and pail bumped into him, the ensign asked him in a harsh, authoritative tone, "Where are you going, sailor?" The man replied, "I'm going to mop the floor, sir." The ensign snorted, "You'd better learn naval terminology, sailor. You're not going downstairs to mop the floor; you're going below to swab the deck."

Wearily, but respectfully the sailor replied, "I'll try to remember sir." To which the ensign snarled back, "You'd better, sailor, If I ever hear you say "downstairs again' I'll throw you out that little round window over there."

Christian communication is a challenge because in the end it is a spiritual discipline. Here are some simple, direct "Dos and Don'ts" I have gleaned from my 32 years as a pastor; many learned through my own regrettable mistakes.

Christian communication:

Seeks to uplift. Glorify and reward good intentions. It does not secretly degrade by letter or words.

It makes criticism a matter of content and not an issue of personalities. It does not make criticism a stage for displaying one's power, superiority in knowledge, or skill in expression.

In public exchanges Christian communication again holds to content, seeking the Christ in all parties no matter what point of view they hold. It does not engage in public expressions which demean others.

Christian communication is honest and expressive. It does not hold back the truth when it needs to be spoken and expressed, but shares it directly and sensitively.

Christian communication forgives and forgets. It does not harangue or fight using innuendo, nor does it simply marshal destructive arguments only to seem right to win a point. Christian communication seeks the truth whether or not it supports his or her position.

Christian communication does not seek to get even.

Christian communication is careful about criticism and does not use it as a helpful expression of love. Communicate love with praise, affirmation, and appreciation. If these words are difficult for you because you are the silent type, then practice them over and over every day until they are not. If they are difficult because you are the "critical type," commit to being another type and seek the help to do so.

We can all use some correction in the way we express things so that we are clearer about what we mean to say. Witness the great surgeon teacher who was discussing a case with a class of medical students and asked," The muscle in the patient's right leg has contracted until it is shorter than that in the left. Therefore, he limps. What would you do in such a circumstance? "

One student quickly raised his hand and said with authority, "I'd limp too."

Loose Lips Sink Ships, the sign in seaside diners and coastal bus stations warned during wartime. Let us remember that they sink relationships with even more regularity. We are called by God to employ the gift of speech to add greater buoyancy to our relationships and the healing truths that bring the love of God to our community.

Holding Onto the Holy

March 5, 2000

There was a short-lived television program which took the concept of exploitation to new depths. The show featured a bevy of attractive women in wedding gowns being paraded before the national TV audience. Each woman was questioned as to why she wanted to be married to a millionaire, and what she would bring to his life. Repeatedly the program host announced that one of these "lucky" women would soon not only have the chance to meet a millionaire, but to marry him that night. I was astonished. I was sure that it was some sort of bad joke.

The millionaire groom was gradually described, with a narration of the accumulation of his wealth and success. Then with great embellishment the millionaire was revealed and introduced to the audience. He carefully looked over the five contestants and made his choice. The program ended with the marriage being performed by a justice of the peace, and the newly married pair left the stage in a cloud of glittering fanfare, supposedly for wedded bliss.

Needless to say, the prince charming story ended within the week. Soon there was dark and troubling information coming to the surface about the pasts of both the millionaire and the contestant who became his wife for a few days. Even more troubling was the sacrilegious intent of the media, which made a travesty of the institution of marriage, the worth of women and the profundity of relationships.

The TV audience grew exponentially as the program continued to air. I wondered what drew the audience to this spectacle. Was it a kind of vicarious pleasure at seeing a real life Prince Charming story played out before their eyes? Or was it disbelief that after all that has been said in this country about preserving the holy ritual of marriage and family, the national angst over the pain and personal dislocation reflected in our divorce rate, they were now witnessing the public degradation of the institution of marriage?

We do not know what happened in the minds and hearts of the creators and producers of this show when they decided to make money on trivializing the sacrament of marriage. But the negative outcry against them made them know that sacrilege can be costly. We can only hope that somehow they also realized the moral implications.

What we can do is use this event to renew some of our own commitment to whatever it is that our faith signifies as being sacred, holy, set apart for special respect and awe. It requires our careful handling and attention because it is sublimely attached to the presence of God. This is an appropriate time to ask ourselves about the nature of the holy and the shape of our response to it.

In the Old Testament, the presence of God was often indicated by the presence of the divine, the holy light, the Shechinah. This shimmering, at times blinding presence of God appeared in the burning bush out of which Moses discerned the voice of God calling him. It appeared again in the glowing cloud and pillar of fire which led the children of Israel in the Exodus. People saw it burning upon the heights of Mt. Sinai where Moses encountered God and delivered the Ten Commandments, the guiding principles of the law. The glowing light was the signature of the holy, stamped into the stone that set forth the conduct of the community of God.

After years of his encounter with the fire of God, people began to notice that the face of Moses itself glowed with the light of the holy, the Shechinah. To them it was an outward manifestation of the holiness which had mysteriously entered this man and come forth in his words, and deeds, and compassion for them.

When the great prophet Elijah was about to leave this life, he asked his understudy, Elisha what he would want to be granted before they were separated. Elisha said that he wanted a double portion of the Shechinah, the holiness or spirit he had experienced in the life of his teacher. This was a request of respect, a statement that said, "If I am to do what you have done, I will need more of what God has given to you."

And when Elijah was taken from Elisha, the story says, he was swept from this dimension of life by the fire of the presence of God, the Shechinah, taking the form of horses and chariots. So it was said that when the day of the Messiah was about to dawn, Moses and Elisha would be returned to earth in the Shechinah.

It is no wonder that both Mark and Matthew tell this story. For their time, it was the sign of the fulfilling of the prophecy of their faith, and the verification that Jesus was that fulfillment. Beyond that it was another remarkable, significant experience with the Shechinah fire of the holy. One interpretation of the intent of Jesus in taking his disciples to the mountain was to prove to them and to all who would hear their words later that he was the fulfillment of the prophecies about the Messiah. But another interpretation of his intent was that, like Elijah, he wanted to pass to them the fire of the holy, so that they would know that what glowed in their lives after he was gone was the same fire of God which had inspired and enlivened his work when he was among them.

The communities of faith, established by the Apostles and evangelists has spent two millennia discerning where the Shechinah, the light of the holy appears in our lives. And in those 2000 years we have come to some conclusions, which are worth reviewing.

Let us remember that life itself is holy. When the face of Moses glowed and when Jesus the man was wrapped in holy fire, we were alerted that the fire of God dwells in human beings. John said it clearly when he said the Kingdom of God is within you. Peter speaks of it when he refers to the morning star, which rises in the hearts of mere mortals. This is why Rome had such problems recruiting Christians to serve in her armies that were trying to suppress and conquer the wild tribes of Northern Europe. The followers of Jesus believed that just as Jesus had seen in them the Shechinah, and in his death and resurrection given witness to its power, they saw in all humans, Romans or "barbarians," that same glow of God and would not desecrate it with wonton destruction.

This is why we have such a hard time with the issue of abortion. For those who believe that a human life begins with conception, abortion is a desecration of life. For those who believe that human life begins with the start of brain waves, or during the second trimester, the forcing of women to carry an unwanted pregnancy to birth without a choice is a desecrating blow to the autonomy of their beings.

So it is when a man and a woman make a sacred vow to be joined in marriage. We consider this a sacred act, a time in which the glow of the holy is heightened in a relationship because of the commitments to each other. The family which is produced by this union is likewise recognized as filled with the sacred, and the holy. That is why we baptize children. We do not do it to add to what the children already bring into the world; we do it in order to recognize the holiness God has put into their flesh and blood. We re-commit to telling the story of this holiness in our children's lives through our words and deeds as the family of their birth, and the family of their faith.

So the respect of marriage is the same respect we have for life. The wedding service which we perform in our church reflects the gravity of our respect for the holy which rises to the surface in a relationship when it says: "This estate should not be entered into lightly, or with selfish motives, but prayerfully." It then declares to all who witness the event, "Let marriage be held in honor among all."

It is the poignant presence of this eternal holiness in a marriage service, which makes us, weep, pass out, tremble, and become tongue-tied. It is worth preserving in our services of marriage and in other rituals in our lives where the holy is present and acknowledged. It is worth remembering when a marriage painfully breaks up. We should never make light of these painful situations, and only involve ourselves in that which heals and helps. And certainly we should not be involved in anything which makes a public spectacle of this pain for profit.

Respect and awe for the holy ought to extend to our respect for the sanctity of relationships which are not marriage relationships. We should respect relationships and their abilities to amplify the holy fires which burn in the human soul. To seek to destroy friendships, and to not take seriously the loyalty, responsibility and caring they require of us is a desecration of the holy. When we repeat hurtful comments, whether true or untrue, which erodes a friendship for no reason save selfish gain or satisfaction; it is a desecration of the holiness of friendship.

Respect for the holy should extend to all relationships and covenants. There is much to be improved in the relationship between a worker and an employer in this country and the world. The employer/employee relationships of our past were as fraught with trouble as they are today.

When my sneakers are sold to me at dirt-cheap prices because a company works children in Asian sweatshops without safety equipment and considerations we would demand for workers in this county, there is something wrong with this; something unholy with the worker/employer covenant and respect for life itself.

I recently attended a conference of people from the biological sciences who are contractors with the Department of Energy working on genome sequencing. I was amazed by the work of Dr. Sallie Chisolm and her colleagues who are attempting to sequence the genome of a tiny one celled microorganism called *prochlorococcus*. This microorganism inhabits the temperate and tropic zones of our oceans. Fifteen years ago its existence was unknown to humans. After a few years of study it was determined that there are more of these microorganisms than there are human cells in all humans on earth, and makes up a majority of the biomass. Its role in processing CO_2 in and out of our atmospheres is a key component in the changes in our weather. In discovering that an infusion of iron into its environment would cause this organism to reproduce at an incredible rate and to thrive immensely, one scientist said, "Give me a tanker filled with powdered iron and I'll give you the next ice age." Apparently this joke was not so far off from the truth.

I noticed that as Dr. Chislom described this organism and asked that its genome be sequenced so that we could better understand it and its unique processes of photosynthesis, she disclosed an awe and respect of its humble being. When someone in the audience suggested that the genetic code of this cell could be tweaked and then the organism returned to the ocean to test the effect over a controlled area, she balked. Her answer was: "Well the ocean and these animals have been working pretty well for three billion years, and I don't want to mess with it."

Dr. Chislom's words also demonstrated a kind of holy respect for both the forces of the sea, and the glow of life in this simple, yet fascinatingly complex little organism. Because of her awareness of the holy she was not willing to use it as though it were just an object to be casually manipulated.

The holy breaks forth in phenomena all around us. If we allow ourselves to view life as Jesus did, as the Apostles did, and as many generations of the faithful have done for thousands of years, we can find the holy everywhere. The history of our world lets us know the folly of believing that the holy can be used to lead armies of religious oppression, justify the cruel and the violent, and wield abusive power over others.

When it arises let us never exploit it, denigrate it with mindless dalliances, self indulgent endeavors or ridiculous television programs. Let us do as Moses did, and take off our shoes and walk upon the blessed ground with our bare flesh willing to absorb its heat, and minds willing to take in its eternal personification.

I really love fishing

Is Sorry Enough?

September 15, 2002

What would have happened if one of the perpetrators of the September 11th attack on the World Trade Center had miraculously survived? And what would have happened if during his incarceration it was discovered that he was deeply remorseful about what he had done? Imagine that during that period of deep remorse he repeatedly poured out his anguished apology for a heinous mistake in judgment, a mistake that he would painfully carry to his grave. If your spouse, or child, or someone you loved, had died in one of the attacks, what would you do if he begged to be forgiven? Could you and would you pardon him?

Lewis B. Smedes wrote a book called *The Art of Forgiving.* In it he presents his readers with a similar case: Some people have said 'forgiveness' can be dangerous and immoral. Simon Wiesenthal's stunning story in 'The Sun Flower,' is the story of how he walked away and left a young SS trooper to die unforgiven when he was in the concentration camp in Mauthausen, Austria. The soldier lay dying from head wounds and begged Wiesehthal to forgive him. But Wiesenthal walked away.

Wiesenthal was a young architect at the time, sure that he was doomed along with the other Jews caught in Hitler's death machine. On a certain afternoon, he was given the job of cleaning out rubbish from an improvised hospital outside the camp where wounded German soldiers were trucked in from the Russian front. Toward evening, a nurse took him by the arm and brought him to the bedside of a boyish storm trooper named Karl, whose head was bandaged with pus-soaked bandages. He would soon die.

Karl grabbed Wiesenthal's wrist. He whispered that he had to talk to a Jew before he died so that he could confess some terrible things that he had done to Jews and be forgiven for them. He confessed what he had done while he was stationed in the Russian village of Dnepropetrovsk. His company was ordered to take reprisals in the village. They packed a frame house with Jews, including many children, poured gasoline on the floors, locked the doors, and set the house on fire. People near the windows jumped. The soldiers shot them before they landed on the ground. They shot the little children right along with the parents, machine-gunned them in the air as they fell. Karl finished his confession and appeared to be weeping, and then, when he got control of himself, he begged Wiesenthal to forgive him. He could not die in peace unless a Jew forgave him for the terrible things he did in Dnepropetrovsk.

Wiesenthal listened, awestruck, to everything Karl told him. He said nothing. Finally he yanked his hand away and left Karl to die with his unforgivable sins unforgiven.

Afterward Wiesenthal worried that maybe it had been wrong not to forgive a young man who begged for forgiveness on his deathbed. When the war was over, and Wiesenthal had survived the Holocaust, he wrote his story. At the end of it he asked his readers, "Was my silence at the bedside of the dying Nazi right or wrong?" This is a profound moral question that challenges the conscience. What would you have done?

Publishers of "The Sun Flower" sought answers to Wiesenthal's question from a range of distinguished people and published their replies. Here are some samples of what they said.

▪ You would never have been able to live with yourself had you forgiven him. I would have strangled him.

▪ We cannot forgive murderers.

▪ I believe you followed a proper and honest path.

▪ To forgive everything means that one is lacking in discrimination, in true feeling, in reasonableness, in memory.

▪ One cannot and should not go around happily killing and torturing and then when the Moment has come, simply ask and receive forgiveness.

▪ I believe that the easy forgiving of such crimes perpetuates the evil it wants to alleviate.

Instead of Karl, we write in the name of our imaginary terrorist, or the name of the terrorist who helped plan 911 and was captured after a gun battle in Pakistan.

Should we forgive if either of them asks for it? Should the people directly hurt by the terrorist planning forgive the planner if he begs to be forgiven?

While we ponder this, let's look carefully at the words from the gospel of Matthew. In this account Jesus had been telling the disciples how they should handle the case of a believer who had wronged them. Hearing Jesus' sage advice on confronting the person and trying to settle things with the help of objective input from other believers, he wondered aloud just how many times he should go through this ritual of forgiveness when someone continued to wrong him. "How many times should I forgive," he asked.

"Seventy times seven," Jesus said. In the vernacular of the day that phrase meant 'endlessly'. There is no set number of times you should consider forgiving a person who honestly and earnestly seeks pardon for what he or she has done. Jesus goes on to tell a parable to emphasize the meaning of forgiveness in the sight of God.

The parable recounts the day that a king decided to settle accounts with all of the slaves to whom he had advanced money. The account books prominently revealed the debt of a slave who owed him an incredible amount of money. The amount listed in the text was ten thousand talents.

Several years ago a man named Arland Hultgren calculated just how big the slave's debt was in modern terms. He pointed out that when General Motors of North America had a work force of 170,478 the annual payroll of that company was comparable to the 10,000 talents in first century purchasing power. So the slave owed a bit more than it would have taken to employ a fully equipped army for a year. It is no wonder that when he was brought before the king he said that he could not pay the debt.

And as was the custom of the day, the king started proceedings to have the slave and his family sold so that he could recoup some tiny part of what it was costing him to carry the slave's debt. The slave was distraught at what was about to happen to him and those he loved because of his incredible financial irresponsibility. He fell to his knees and begged, "Have patience with me, and I will pay you everything."

It is clear that there is no way this slave was going to pay everything back to his master. The king must have had great trust in the slave's abilities at one time because the king had entrusted the slave with an incredible amount of wealth and value. Having squandered a king's ransom, how could he beg for patience and promise to repay?

But the Master took pity upon the slave. Not only did he release the slave and his family from the intention to sell them all, but he also forgave the debt!

Later, the slave comes upon a fellow slave who had borrowed money from him. The debt he is owed amounts to about four months of pay in first century purchasing power. It seems our forgiven slave is really upset that this debtor is avoiding paying him. Incensed by his fellow slave who has not paid him; the man grabs the debtor by the throat and angrily demands payment. The assailed debtor pleads in the same words the first slave used when confronted by his king, "Have patience with me and I will pay you." The difference in the two cases of the debts is that the first slave owed such an incredible amount that there was no way on earth that he could repay. In this second case, the debtor could have found a payment plan that would have worked, given a little patience by the debt holder.

When the king found out about the dispute and that the forgiven slave had tossed the other slave into debtor's prison, the king was not happy. He called the slave to account and had him put into the same debtor's prison with the other slave.

The sentiment of this parable is repeated by other passages that commemorate the teachings of Jesus. At the end of the Lord's Prayer in Matthew 6, Jesus reiterates what he has said in the prayer, presumably to make us understand that he means what he says. He says, "For if you forgive others their trespasses, your heavenly Father will also forgive you; but if you do not forgive others, neither will your Father forgive your trespasses."

When Jesus was crucified and had every right to shout out his rage over the injustice that was being perpetrated against him, instead he prayed for the angry mob around him, saying, "Father, forgive them, they don't know what they are doing."

There is another parable about sin and forgiveness and repentance. It is told in Paul Wharton's book called *Stories and Parables for Preachers and Teachers.*

Two men once visited a holy man to ask his advice. "We have done wrong actions," they said, "and our consciences are troubled. Can you tell us what we must do so that we may be forgiven and feel clear of our guilt?"

"Tell me your wrong-doings, my sons," said the old man.

The first man said, "I have committed a great and grievous sin." "What about you?" the holy man asked the second.

"Oh," he said, "I have done quite a number of wrong things, but they are all quite small and not at all important."

The holy man considered the matter for a while. "This is what you must do", he said at last. "Each of you must go and bring me a stone for each of his misdeeds."

The first man returned carrying an enormous boulder. The boulder was so heavy that he could hardly lift it, and with a groan he let it fall at the feet of the holy man. Along came the second man, cheerfully carrying a bag of small pebbles. This he also lay at the feet of the saint.

"Now," said the holy man, "take all these stones and put them back where you found them." The first man shouldered his rock again, and staggered back to the place from which he had brought it. But the second man could only remember where a few of his pebbles had lain.

After some time, the second man came back and said that the task was too difficult.

> You must know, my son that sins are like these stones. If a man has committed a great sin, it lies heavy on his conscience; but if he is truly sorry, he is forgiven and the load is taken away. But if a man is constantly doing small things that are wrong, he does not feel any very great load of guilt and so is not sorry and remains a sinner. So you see, it is as important to avoid little sins as big ones.

When Lewis Smedes pondered the question of forgiving Karl, the young SS trooper who begged Wiesenthal to forgive his genocidal murder of innocent Jews, he was afraid that if he were to counsel forgiveness he would do so for the wrong reasons. Smedes said that he would not consider it right to offer forgiveness when he was just trying to make dying easier for a young man who was in a pitiable condition. He said, "I feared I would have spoken forgiving words just to protect my own conscience." He would not want to live with the memory of refusing to forgive a dying man.

What was clear to Smedes, and us, was that we were not the injured party. Wiestenthal was himself a prisoner of the German Reich, daily watching his people brutalized by people like Karl. He was now being asked to rise above his suffering and grant solace to one who was causing the suffering. It was too much for Wiesanthal. He refused. Yet later, he revisited the scene over and over. Obviously something still bothered him about what had happened.

Smedes writes, "I hoped, however, that I would have had the wisdom to tell Karl that I had no right to forgive him on behalf of the people he murdered. But I also hoped I would have had faith to invite him to join me in asking God to forgive him."

So what would I have done if I had been a chaplain, representing our faith to all the Karls of the world? Would I be expected to offer consoling words of God's forgiveness of young Karl? Would I be expected as the representative of Christ to accept his confession and grant him absolution in the eyes of God, if not in the eyes of those he killed and their families?

One line of thought warns us against cheap grace. It is cheapening of the commandments of our faith to just let someone sin and say, "I'm sorry" and that's the end of it. The other line of thought says that forgiveness isn't a cheap commodity at all. There is a personal cost to its application. That is why it is so precious and why we so value the way God forgives us. It is a measure of our faith. It is a measure of us.

Karl is before you. Shall we grant him pardon and absolution in death? How would you counsel Wiesanthal?

From my teen years to my thirties

Thy Kingdom Come

August 21, 2005

Mark 1:9-14

Matthew 6:25-33

In his ministry, Jesus talks frequently about the Kingdom of God. Most of the parables begin with him saying, "The Kingdom of God is like...." And here, at the beginning of his mission, when he says, "the time is fulfilled," he refers to the Kingdom of God. "The Kingdom of God has come near," he says. It is "at hand." It is here, with us, within us, around us, among us.

And yet the Kingdom of God has been one of the least understood and most infrequently mentioned aspects of Jesus' ministry. Often there has been a tendency in the church to remove the Kingdom of God to some other, distant time or place. Many locate the Kingdom of God in the far future, the time of the Second Coming perhaps, or where you go when you die. Some would refer to the Kingdom of God as the eventual result of human progress to which we are growing ever closer. All these ideas put the Kingdom conveniently, not here, as Jesus says, but somewhere else.

It was Karl Marx who made the famous quip about religion being the "opiate of the masses." He meant that he saw religion used as a narcotic to keep the masses under control. They were told to work hard, obey their masters, put off gratification, and most importantly, to stop complaining about injustice and exploitation. According to Marx, religion promised them a reward in heaven. Meanwhile, their masters got their reward here and now, based on the wealth generated by docile labor. In this view, the Kingdom of God is a myth perpetrated by the ruling class to keep the workers repressed.

That is not what Jesus had in mind when he said "the Kingdom of God is at hand." It is that element of immediacy that keeps the Kingdom of God from being a fantasy. If we believe it is "at hand," the Kingdom of God becomes a powerful, dangerous and threatening notion. Think about it. Jesus comes with a message that says there is another, better world, one that will replace this one. Indeed, his proclamation is that this replacement has already started with his coming.

As we know, both by common sense and from the story of King Herod when Jesus was born, the news of another Kingdom or a new king makes the present king very nervous. Hence, if you're happy with the "kingdom" you're in — that is, your social, political, economic, or even intellectual, artistic, moral, or emotional arrangement — you don't want to hear about some other, new order.

For many centuries, the church was invested in the stability of the Roman Empire, or whatever other government or regime prevailed. Frankly, it was not in the church's interest to highlight Jesus' talk about any other Kingdom. It was better to relegate God's Kingdom to the end of time, or the end of life, or the far future, than to deal with anything that might even imply upsetting the established order.

But Jesus does not say the Kingdom of God is coming someday. He does not point beyond himself, to some other time and place when the Kingdom will arrive. He does not locate the Kingdom in the distant future.

The Kingdom of God, whatever it is, is accessible and available today. That is the primary truth Jesus talks about. In the gospel of John, Jesus is even more succinct: He himself is the Kingdom, the Way, the Truth, and the Life of the world.

This is a huge challenge to the conventional and accepted way of doing things. Jesus' teaching about the Kingdom of God stresses the difference between our present, secular existence and the Kingdom. The values, loyalties, actions, behavior, and even the way we think are very different than they will be in God's Kingdom. Jesus presents a contrast between God's Kingdom and the kingdoms of this world.

Jesus is proclaiming a different reality, a different world, and a new life, when compared to our secular existence, which is partial, false, and defective. He asks us to look at the way we live and to understand that it need not be this way.

This must have been a profoundly hopeful message to people at the bottom of the social order, which would have been most of the people who heard him. It was a promise readily embraced even by people crippled by their own guilt over real and imagined sin.

Jesus proclaims the infiltration of one world into another; he affirms the beginning of a new world and the end of the old. It reminds me of a song by the band, REM, from a few years ago: "It's the end of the world as we know it... and I feel fine."

For most of the people to whom Jesus ministered it was a world of oppression, injustice, exploitation, violence, illness, suffering, and death. It was a world in which the Romans controlled everything for the enrichment of themselves and their wealthy clients. It was a sad existence for conquered and subject people. It was a life of dislocation, poverty, and abuse. The news that this sorrowful world was ending, its time fulfilled, and that a new world was arriving, was greeted with eager anticipation by some, and with fear and anxiety by others.

Nearly everything that Jesus did makes this truth real and visible to us. Not just his parables, but his healings also serve to illustrate the new and different reality now available. Perhaps more convincing are the exorcisms he performed, driving out evil spirits and demons. He confirmed that the present world, where such malignant entities have destructive power over people, is fading fast. He defeated those powers and principalities, and released us for new life in God's Kingdom.

Not even Karl Marx was this revolutionary. Marx's utopia was relegated to the future, to arrive after prolonged class-struggle. It failed, because his followers thought they could bring about his utopia by violence. In the end, his philosophy was as much an "opiate of the people" as the religion he criticized, because it removed liberation, peace, justice, and love to some theoretical future, while in the meantime his movement was all about war. Jesus knows that people cannot institute the Kingdom of God by themselves, least of all by violence against others. The Kingdom of God is something God makes real now, beginning in the human heart.

Some will say that we need to fight fire with fire. But I know of no one who, upon discovering a fire in the kitchen, will fight it by starting another fire in the living room. No; we fight fire with water, we fight evil with good, and we fight darkness with light. When Jesus proclaims the presence of the Kingdom of God it is to oppose injustice, decay and corruption by their opposites: justice, righteousness and life.

We cannot bring peace by terror and we cannot use injustice to bring justice; we cannot bring goodness by doing evil; we cannot uplift the poor by making the rich richer; we cannot make ourselves more secure by inspiring fear; we cannot bring about love by hate. Jesus rejected all earthly means, strategies and tactics to achieve his ends. For him the end and the means were identical. We will realize the Kingdom of God by living according to the values of the Kingdom of God, here and now.

This is what Paul means when he says, "Our citizenship," or "our commonwealth," "is in heaven" (*Philippians 3:20*). We are citizens or subjects of God's heavenly Kingdom, even as we still live and work and play in earthly principalities. Peter uses the same imagery when he says we are aliens and exiles in the world (*1 Peter 2:11*). We live in one world, but we are citizens of another. It is that other world that shapes our values, habits, actions, words, thoughts, and loyalties.

A popular movie, often shown on cable TV is *The Matrix*. In this film, the protagonist, a hacker named Neo, discovers that the world we think we live in is an elaborate virtual reality computer program into which we are all plugged. True reality is different. Most of the Earth has been destroyed and the ruins are inhabited by machines that enslave unconscious people and suck energy out of them.

It is a profoundly spiritual movie because it depicts the truth about there being two worlds and that the world in which we live is, in some ways, an illusion, or projection. That much is true. Where Jesus differs is when he says that it is the other world, the Kingdom of God, is perfect, blessed, and good. That is the real world. That is the world God made and intended for us.

The Matrix makes an error we all make. When we talk about living in "the real world," we usually mean that we need to lose our innocence and fantasies, and recognize that the world is a tough place. Jesus says just the opposite. The world we have made is the tough place. The world perverted by sin, death and evil is the world we, in our brokenness have invented for ourselves.

Jesus' good news is that it doesn't have to be this way. In truth, it isn't this way at all. The Kingdom of God is not far off. It is at hand, it is within, and it is among us right now. It is the real world. It is the true world.

Jesus is the doorway into the true life. We enter into God's Kingdom through him, by believing in him, by trusting in and obeying him, and by living as he shows us how to live.

In *The Matrix*, Neo is given a choice. If he takes one pill he can stay in his unconscious existence, never the wiser. But if he takes the other pill he will wake up to see and know the truth. Faith in Jesus is like this second pill; except, we do not wake up to the horror of a world destroyed by war. The opposite happens. We realize that the war, and the horror, and the destruction, are rooted in lies. The real world is the Kingdom of God, where justice, righteousness, goodness, peace, and truth prevail.

That is where we need to follow Jesus. It is the Kingdom of God, and it is here.

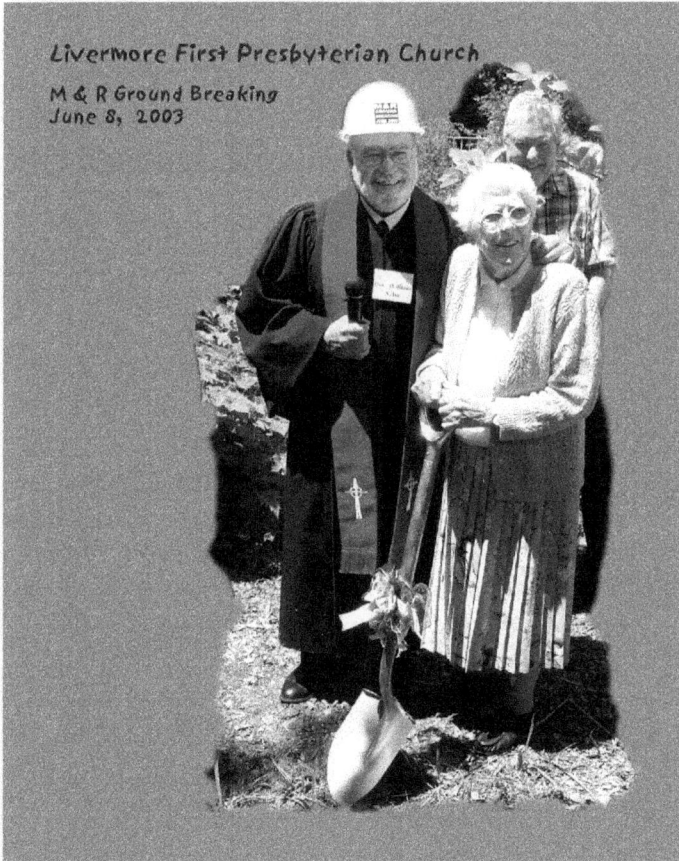

*Henrietta Greer and Ralph Greenlee help me
break ground for the church renovation*

Tumbleweeds in the Fence of Christmas

December 1, 2002

Sometime in 1877 the first tumbleweed was discovered in Bon Homme County, South Dakota. It was a strange weed to find there because the plant was known as Russian Thistle and was native to the arid steppes of the Ural Mountains in Russia. Apparently it had sprung up as the result of stray seeds that had hitchhiked to the United States in a load of flax seed imported by Ukrainian farmers. Twenty years later it had tumbled into a dozen states and by 1900, it had reached the Pacific Coast.

The spread of tumbleweeds was greatly aided by farmers who removed prairie grasses, creating a perfect environment, smooth and flat, for a plant that could roll across the landscape dispersing its seeds. With each plant carrying over a quarter of a million seeds, able to germinate and grow where they were dropped, the tumbleweed became a problem to the American range.

As farmers enclosed more and more of the open range with barbed wire, after its invention in 1874, they found that each year the number of tumbleweeds increased in the wire fencing. It also became obvious that the worst thing anyone could do with these weeds, some as large as Volkswagens, was to free them from the fences and let them tumble on across the next parcel of open range. Whether that land was one's own or a neighbor's, the results were the same. New weeds were planted and grew to interfere with farming. As time went on, each line of fence became something of a barrier to the loose, tumbling, Russian Thistle weed-spreading machine. They found that burning the tumble weeds was the only way they could prevent them from dispersing to the next open range.

The Christmas season is in many ways like a line of barbed wire fence strung across the range lands of our lives. It catches all sorts of emotional and spiritual baggage that has been blowing through our lives all year long. It allows us some time to look and decide if it is something we should let tumble into the range of next year, or pull it off of the fence and burn it.

The tumbleweeds of spiritual and emotional distress that can be found piled against the wire fences of the Christmas season encompass three topics: Love, death, and money.

When I was a young child, my foster parents were clever at keeping me clear about the fact that Santa was going to come and deliver delightful presents to our house. I had no doubt that all-knowing Santa saw me as a good little boy and would not pass me by with his gifts. What my foster parents couldn't do was assure me that my father loved me enough to be able to communicate to me the "joy" of the season. A divorce had put us at such a distance, that I was unable to hear or feel whatever love he felt for me. Each Christmas I tried to receive it, like a traveler in a far off country straining to hear a familiar radio station through the static transmission of distance. Increasingly, Christmas, that season so good at catching in its grasp all of the life experiences of the dying year, had become the time when the trouble with the love of my Dad stopped tumbling and allowed me to really look at it.

The negative knots of love, anger, resentment, and yearning for nurture, balled up into a tumbleweed of doubt and disappointment, had been blowing across my little life all year. It was throwing seeds each time my Dad failed to show up, or made our visit too short. At Christmas, the Dad issue was stuck in the wire, and each year I had to pull it free. For most of my young life I simply tossed it aside with tears of resentment and let it drift into the range of the next year.

My father disappeared from my life all together by the time I was in the third grade. From then on, and even after his death, I continued to sort the vestiges of resentment blown into the wire of Christmas and toss them to the winds blowing across the year to come.

The unresolved issues with Dad continued to plant seeds of trouble in other places. It showed up in the way I trusted or didn't trust people with love and devotion. It showed up in what made me unnecessarily, and often unfairly angry with others. It showed up in my relationship with my wife and children, with my work and my play. Sometimes they were little tumbleweeds, sometimes larger plants. But each was a plant of spiritual disturbance that choked out love and personal connection wherever they chanced to grow and proliferate.

A few years ago, I decided it was time to end the "Dad thing." It was time to look at the tumbleweed, to burn it with forgiveness, understanding, and compassion for whatever Dad did or didn't do. Following the example of the love of Christ, the great incarnation we celebrate at Christmas, I piled up all the thorny, Dad stuff and torched it. And each year I notice that less and less of it grows anywhere in the succeeding year. It has been a great relief.

Look to the wire line strung across your lives this Christmas. Are there tumbleweeds of trouble piled up there that you need to gather and burn in the love and compassion of the Christ child? Are you finding as you patrol this fence line and pause there, you find residue of the weedy way you have dealt with the loves of your lives? In one section of fence you may discover the knot of jealousy you have fused with the love of your brother or sister, or good friend. In another, you may find the overly impatient expectation you have mixed into the love of your children, or the overly sensitive needs you have combined with the love of your spouse or sweetheart. Tear them loose and cast them to the winds and they will blow across your year yet another season, planting their trouble many places that will ultimately afflict you and others.

How long will the memory of the spouse who left you, the lover who betrayed you, the parent who abandoned you, and all the other hurtful experiences, pile up against your fence each Christmas? This is the time to patrol the fence, armed with the burning fire of the love of Christ, the forgiving maturity of God's grace which is showered upon the human condition. Each time we meet these knots of tangled love issues, we can set them ablaze with the loving wisdom that redeems us from the fate of planting them again, and being obstructed by their thorny presence in our lives.

Christmas is a time to examine the things that trouble our spirit; the anxiety that threatens to fill the range of the year to come with unresolved problems with love, death and possessions. Let the Christ child become the Risen Christ whose fiery grace can consume resentment, disappointment, self-doubt, self-consuming anger, and selfish desire.

Don't tumble along with the tumbling tumbleweeds this Christmas season. Gather them at the fence, and burn them in the great hope of the new season and a new life.

Amen.

Acknowledgements

Augustus, Cyrus; "Nouns and Adverbs," from *A 4ᵗʰ Course of Chicken Soup for the Soul*; by Jack Canfield, et.al.; Heath Communications Inc.; 1997

Barclay, William; *The Letters of John and Jude*; Westminster/John Knox; 2002

Hewitt, James; *Illustrations Unlimited*; Tyndall House Publications, Wheaton, IL, 1988

Nouwen, Henri; *Gracias: A Latin American Journal*; Harpercollins; 1983

Lectionary; "Homiletics"; March 2000

Schuller, Robert; *Turning Hurts into Halos*; Thomas Nelson; 2000

Smedes, Lewis; *The Art of Forgiving*; Ballantine Books, 1996

Wharton, Paul; *Stories and Parables for Preachers and Teachers;* Abington Press; 1986

Rev. William (Bill) E. Nebo was born in Los Angeles County, California. Bill attended the University of California at Los Angeles and graduated with a Bachelor's Degree in Philosophy in 1960. After studying at the San Francisco Theological Seminary where he earned his Master of Divinity degree, he was ordained in the Presbytery of Los Angeles in 1968. He served at the First United and Portalhurst Presbyterian Churches as Assistant Pastor until 1972. After serving for four years as an assistant and associate pastor at the Livermore Presbyterian Church in Livermore, California, he became its senior pastor and remained there until his retirement in 2006.

He was married for thirty years to his partner, Jean and they had two children, Valerie and Christopher. After Jean's death he married Jane Sheridan who brought her two sons, Kursten and Justen, into their life together. In addition to granddaughter Anna Jean, the Nebos have been blessed with additional grandchildren, Isaac Stanley and Aaliyah Elizabeth.

Bill has and continues to have an abiding interest in bioethics and sits on the Institutional Review Board of Lawrence Livermore National Laboratory, the Bioethics Committee and Institutional Review Board of Valley Care Hospital, and the Human Subjects of Research Working Group of the Department of Energy.

Bill is author of the book, *The Soul's Journey, Best Loved Sermons*.